INNOVATION

IN WORLD MISSION

DEREK T. SEIPP

INNOVATION

IN WORLD MISSION

A Framework for
Transformational Thinking
about the Future of World
Mission

WILLIAM CAREY
LIBRARY

Innovation in World Mission: A Framework for Transformational Thinking about the Future of World Mission

Published by William Carey Library
1605 E. Elizabeth St. | Pasadena, CA 91104 | www.missionbooks.org

Emily Pham, copyeditor
Hugh Pindur, graphic design
Rose Lee-Norman, indexer

William Carey Library is a ministry of
Frontier Ventures | www.frontierventures.org

Printed in the United States of America
20 19 18 17 16   5 4 3 2 1 BP300

Library of Congress Cataloging-in-Publication Data

Names: Seipp, Derek T., author.
Title: Innovation in world mission : a framework for transformational
    thinking about the future of world mission / Derek T. Seipp.
Description: Pasadena, CA : William Carey Library, 2016. | Includes
    bibliographical references and index.
Identifiers: LCCN 2016008757 (print) | LCCN 2016012365 (ebook) | ISBN
    9780878083978 (pbk.) | ISBN 0878083979 | ISBN 9780878086832 (eBook)
Subjects: LCSH: Missions—Theory. | Change—Religious aspects.
Classification: LCC BV2063 .S39 2016 (print) | LCC BV2063 (ebook) | DDC
    266—dc23

LC record available at http://lccn.loc.gov/2016008757

CONTENTS

FOREWORD

INNOVATE WELL OR FAIL

Derek Seipp, who I am privileged to work with in our Act Beyond leadership team, is correct: mission teams /organizations will either innovate or be impotent in today's challenging global environment. As an airplane flies directly into the opposing winds in order to achieve flight, mission leaders must leverage these swirling realities rather than being defeated. "Global trends" have always been against God's mission—and yet, Jesus brilliantly designed his "disciple making assembly" (*ekklesia* or *church*) to overcome the challenges and launch whole movements which change whole cultures.

FROM STRATEGIC DRIFT TO MULTIPLICATION

This work raises possibilities which can help remove the shackles of traditional mission thinking in the emphasis that "continuous transformation can create a multiplier effect in which changes cascade out in multiple directions" (Seipp, *Innovation in World Mission*, 45). In a sense, this study is a radical return to transformative multiplication noted in Acts 19:10 where the whole Roman Province of Asia (15 million people) heard the word of the Lord within two years. Understanding both the possibility and the necessity of having multiplicative impact is a needed corrective to the huge strategic drift in missions. Some organizations have heeded this call and moved dramatically into the future with exponential impact.

Implications of this work's challenge to correct one's assumptions include:

1.) *Assumption 1:* The church's purpose is merely to worship, disciple, teach and pray—but entities must be created outside the church to bring social justice.

Mission Result: *Evangelism* and *social justice* remain dichotomized and multi-national entities are created to focus on earthly social justice—and in effect usurp or rob the fledgling churches of the God-given role to serve and change its own society in word and deed.

Corrected Assumption: The ekklesia (groups of *obeyers,* not just *converts)* is God's chosen agent to disciple all *ethne* by worshipping, feeding the poor, healing the sick, prayer, helping the widow, casting out demons, doing good business, etc. This exponential impact of *ekklesia* would cut off the roots of systemic issues (e.g. sexual abuse, alcoholism, joblessness, family dysfunction, etc.) as *ekklesia* charges the gates of hell to rescue trapped people.

2.) *Assumption 2:* The first century was an unsophisticated, simplistic time and what occurred in the Book of Acts cannot handle the complexities and pluralism of today's world.

Mission Result: We create and continually test unproven mission strategies rather than using Jesus' approach which changed millions within a few short years

Corrected Assumption: The first century was as challenging, complicated, multi-cultural, and multi-religious as this century is. Religious pluralism and hedonistic philosophies, caused as much persecution of the church then as today. In spite of this complexity, whole societies were discipled. This exponential impact on whole societies is still possible today.

Isaiah 43 is cited below as a reminder to forget former things and see the new things—which include *a way in the desert and streams in the wasteland.* Mission must return to the corrected assumption that whole societies can be dramatically changed—if our organizations will dramatically change. Like Moses, we need to listen to Jethro, "You will never care for everyone's needs this way. Let me show you a better way" (Exodus 18:17–23).

S. Kent Parks, PhD
president / CEO, Beyond (formerly *Mission to Unreached Peoples*)
senior associate for Least Reached Peoples on the Lausanne Committee on World Evangelization

Creation companies do new things more effectively, and they create new models. The key to success in creation companies is creation, not control. (2001, 35)

The Industrial Age organization was marked by hierarchy and control, top down administration. The Information Age is marked by networks, not control, but collaboration. As the global church emerges and spreads to the North, East, and West, let us pray that out of our diversity we will also experience the unity that Jesus prayed for in his high priestly prayer. What if the world saw the unity of the body—unity achieved, not as a goal to be gained, but as a byproduct of an obedience to be demonstrated?

William R. O'Brien

INTRODUCTION

Now abides the past, the present, and the future. But the greatest of these is ...?
What a question to ask the church.

Futurist professor, Peter Bishop, talks about a cone of plausible futures. He
states the future is many, not one.

Research on the issues of aging is rapidly developing in Japan, Singapore,
and the UK. They are learning there is no one cure or solution which will work
for everyone.

Dr. John Anderson, former director of the Advanced Concept division of
NASA, developed a process he called Horizon Mission Methodology. He took scientists so far into the future they could not simply extrapolate past breakthroughs.

Why have mission agencies and associations allowed themselves to arrive at
what Derek Seipp calls a "strategic drift?" Change occurred all around them. The
gap between their methodologies that always worked before, and the dominating
religious, economic, geopolitical, and cultural realities that call for a new way of
seeing and acting seems un-bridge-able. It is a sad day when mission adminis-
trators and practitioners suffer from Anton's Syndrome—a condition marked by
being blind to one's own blindness.

The mega-trends that Seipp identifies, when seen as a whole, create a "mega
context" that challenge missiological thinking. In fact, it is so huge and creates
such a cacophony of sound and fury that it can flip the breaker in our reticular
activating systems.

Taking a cue from Issachar, Seipp calls for leaders who understand the times
and know what to do about it. That calls for faith-based innovation. Which in
turn, calls for research that is appropriate, as long as the research is accurately
focused and not trying to conjure up answers for questions that are not being
asked, or are irrelevant. Seipp does not try to predict the future of world mission,
but shows the way to use scenarios to build some plausible futures.

Tom McGehee talks about "compliance companies" versus "creation companies." Repetition, predictability, and risk-avoidance mark compliance companies.

CHAPTER 1

INNOVATION AND OUR CHANGING WORLD

"A wonderful future awaits . . ." Psalm 37:37 (NLT)

The world is changing. We can see it. We can feel it. Technology is impacting everything we do. The world is becoming increasingly secular. Traditional values seem to be fading. The list goes on and on. The world we were familiar with seems to have vanished. A new world is emerging before our eyes. Even though we deal with a timeless gospel, everything around us is changing. And most of the Christians I know do not welcome these changes.

In 2001, I quit my consulting job in Pittsburgh, PA, entered missionary training school, and moved off to China with my wife to train church planters. During the next twelve years we saw incredible changes in China. In the early days, the Internet, broadband, cell phones, they were all new novelties used by a few privileged individuals. Many of our missionary friends were still struggling to get used to e-mail. It was in China that my wife bought her first cell phone.

In the early days, we could ride bicycles two city blocks and be in the countryside. There, at the edge of the city, it was as if the modern world suddenly stopped and then we jumped fifty or a hundred years back in time. On one side of the street flashy stores carried expensive designer handbags, on the other side of the street, people still carried water buckets suspended from a bamboo poles stretched across their shoulders. When we left that city seven years later, we had to drive twenty minutes just to find any trace of the countryside. When we first moved there, the churches were newborns, struggling for their very survival. Today, these churches are vibrant, mature and growing. Several have ministry expansion plans rivaling those of American churches. The future was unfolding right before our eyes.

When we finally moved back to the states, we thought we were ready for a bit of reverse culture shock, but we were hardly ready for what we found. In only twelve years, American values had changed dramatically. The culture, TV, radio, health care, ideals, social issues, etc.; everything noticeably changed in those twelve years. We could only find shadows of things we remembered; the America we thought we knew, was largely unrecognizable.

We initially blamed it on being away for so long. Yet, we found we were not alone in our feelings. Our friends (who had never left the country) felt their world was largely unrecognizable to them as well. It wasn't just us. We all felt like we were playing catch-up to a strange new world emerging before our eyes. It's also not just America. These same changes are happening on a global scale; impacting every aspect of society, business, government, as well as religious beliefs and practices. The ripple effects are sending tsunamis of change to even the remotest of villages. And if we are to believe the researchers, these changes are only accelerating.

STRATEGIC DRIFT

Our brains are wired to identify familiar patterns. This helps us recognize faces, learn languages, and remember where we placed our car keys. But this also has a detrimental effect for recognizing change as it gives us a tendency to ignore cues that something else is different (Hannagan 2009). Instead, our brains naturally pay attention to the cues that confirm what has remained the same. We have to see changes multiple times before we fully register that a full-blown change has occurred. As a result, change happens faster than we realize. In the meantime, we're fooled into thinking we're safe and don't need to adjust.

Further complicating matters, the projects we manage, the programs we put into effect, and the organizations we lead all have a certain degree of inertia. People are invested financially and mentally to our current plans. Assuming we've fully recognized that change is happening, we have to convince others regarding the impact, and how we should react. Such discussions are often held off until quarterly or annual reviews, yet at those times, so many issues need to be discussed that the issue simply falls off the table. Even if it is, choosing a new strategy and implementing in takes time. Consequently, we react even slower still. You could say our organizations are designed to stay the same.

With our own inherent biases against recognizing the full extent of change, the corrective steps we take usually fall short of what's actually needed (Hannagan 2009). This results in small, but growing gaps between what we actually do and what needs to be done. To make matters worse, these corrections are merely just reactive, rather than proactive in nature. This means we're constantly trailing behind with the changes gaining an increasing lead. It becomes increasingly difficult to adjust activities based on conditions that were true three, five, ten, or even twenty or more years ago. Plans can only be adjusted so much until something entirely different is needed. Still, we constantly try to adapt what we already do to meet new conditions. Hannagan calls this widening gap, strategic drift.

When the Internet first appeared, it was mostly text, with very few images. Telephone companies found they could use analog modems, previously used for text based electronic bulletin boards (remember that loud scratchy sound they made?) to connect users to this new digital world. Speed was slow because the telephone companies used existing capabilities (old twisted copper telephone wires) to respond to new changes in the environment. But, when most of the Internet was just text, fast speeds weren't necessary. Over time, web pages became interactive with rich multimedia, and those copper wires simply couldn't keep up. New, faster modems emerged, but they fell further and further behind the increasing changes. Then came video and YouTube. With diminishing returns, those old capabilities couldn't be tweaked enough to meet emerging needs.

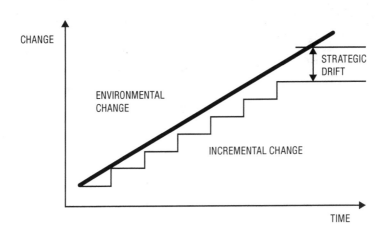

Hannagan, T., *Management: Concepts & Practices* (5th ed.), 2009, 190.

Eventually, those screechy dial-up modems weren't good enough to keep up with what people wanted to do online. Cable companies responded with a much faster technology and people started switching. As the telephone companies increasingly lost customers and revenue, they had to respond. After trying a variety of technologies based on those twisted copper wires, they finally responded by putting superfast fiber optic wires directly into people's homes.

But this is not just about technology. When I was young, I remember singing hymns out of the pew hymnbook. But the emerging Christian contemporary music industry was changing the songs people wanted to sing. Many connected better with emerging praise and worship songs, and they wanted to sing these in church. Soon, there were praise books sitting next to the hymnbooks.

As soon as these praise books were printed, new songs continued to emerge. While the hymnbooks didn't change in decades, within a few years a second praise book appeared next to the hymnal. These songbooks couldn't keep up with the speed at which the new songs were emerging, and buying new songbooks every year was getting expensive for churches. A gap was emerging. Churches started using overhead projectors to shine these songs up on large screens. But this also created a new problem for the music industry that suddenly wasn't selling any new praise books or hymnals. Today, churches don't buy songbooks; they license the right to project the praise song lyrics from the publishers, through a company called CCLI.

Strategic drift eventually increases to the point that the gaps become vast chasms. When that happens, publishing another songbook just doesn't handle the need anymore. An incrementally faster dial-up modem doesn't handle the exponential increase in demand for bandwidth. Existing activities simply fail to meet the changing needs of the environment. As this happens, a wide door of opportunity is open for someone else to suddenly step in and gobble up existing markets, products, and services (Burke 2011). Because the process of drifting away is so gradual, most organizations don't realize the resulting chasm until it's too late. It's the classic boiling frog syndrome: a frog is placed into lukewarm water and the temperature is gradually increased. The frog never recognizes the temperature change and eventually he's cooked alive. We fail to recognize the changes happening around us, and then one day we wake up to find ourselves in a hot pot of boiling water.

Every idea, every product, every plan is vulnerable to strategic drift. Motorola dominated the analog cell phone market in the 90's. When digital cell phone technology emerged, Motorola dismissed it as a fad. Motorola drifted. A chasm formed. Nokia saw the open door and walked through. Within a few years, Nokia cornered the market, and the mighty Motorola was suddenly struggling for survival. Yet, Nokia eventually fell to the same problem. People simply wanted more from their phones. Apple recognized the world had drifted. The iPhone, took over the market. Today, there are signs Apple is struggling with gaps being exploited by ultra-low-cost Android phones. The cycle continues.

World mission is no less immune to these changes. Local churches are engaging overseas, bypassing mission agencies. Churches (knowingly or unknowingly) recognized a gap created by increasing ease of communication and travel. They simply stepped in, and there was nothing malicious about it. The world changed. Many agencies, being heavily invested in their own paradigms, failed to recognize the drift. A chasm formed. A door of opportunity opened and churches walked right through. Most every mission leader I know admits to feeling that new pressures are emerging. People's giving patterns are changing. Young missionaries have different motivations than the previous generation. The mission field itself has changed. Our world is getting smaller. Strategic drift is separating us from being as effective as we could be. How do we fill the chasm? How do we choose the right actions amid such uncertainty? How do we know we'll be relevant in the years ahead? How do we know our actions won't waste kingdom resources?

INNOVATION

Innovation is the process that fills the gap. According to Merriam-Webster, the word innovate means to, "do something in a new way" (Merriam-Webster Dictionary 2014). Because something so radically different is needed to fill the chasm left by strategic drift, the new products seem revolutionary. They often redefine the way an entire sector or industry acts and works. Know this: innovation is not just a fad. In fact the idea isn't new at all.

There are words from antiquity that have been translated "innovate," but our modern word comes from the Latin, *innovates,* which dates to the mid 1500's. Its modern popularity finds its roots in a 1934 book *The Theory of Economic Development* by Joseph Schumpeter. In it, Schumpeter shows how ideas and knowledge are brought together into new combinations, creating new entrepreneurial opportunities. Later, in 1953, Peter Drucker famously stated that innovation and marketing were the "two-and only two-basic functions" of any organization

(Drucker 1954, 32). Mission leaders may do well to write this down, and ponder how it may relate to their organizations as they continue reading this book.

Peter Drucker also said, "In a time of rapid change, the opportunities for improving, for getting results, are also changing rapidly. Things that were impossible or unnecessary yesterday suddenly become possible, and things that made great sense yesterday no longer make sense . . . One of the tasks of leaders is to make sure that we constantly put our scarce resources (people and money) where they do the most good . . . Good intentions are no longer enough" (Hesselbein and Cohen 1999, 53-54).

It might surprise you, but the above quote was *NOT* written for business leaders. He's actually writing to leaders of a non-profit volunteer organization which helps underprivileged inner city youth. His goal was to help the organization find the actions having the greatest impact on literacy and graduation for these youth. Knowing this, you may want to read that again. He continues, "What we have really done is learn the discipline of innovation . . . It means being able and willing to abandon efforts that don't get results-either because we don't know how to produce results or because we are misdirecting our efforts . . . It's not looking at need alone, but looking at need and opportunity . . . We need the discipline of innovation because in a rapidly changing society, our problems are changing" (Hesselbein and Cohen 1999, 55–56).

Innovation is not just a secular fad. It's an important part of our spiritual expression (Oster 2011). "We innovate because we are made to resemble the Great Innovator," says Oster (Oster 2011, Kindle location 562). God created us in his image, and we were created to be creative. When we apply that creativity to work, we simply call it innovation. Genesis shows how early society used God's creative blessing, to innovate in the making of stringed musical instruments, pipes, and bronze and iron tools (Gen 4:21–2). Innovation is God's design.

Innovation needn't be mysterious. Innovation is not something that just comes in a creative spark; it can actually be developed as a discipline (Hesselbein and Cohen 1999, 53–54). It's a way of directing our focus to make the best use of our time, our people, and our resources. And in a rapidly changing world, innovation is all the more necessary.

Over the years, we've learned a lot about how producing innovative ideas. There has been an increasing realization that we cannot merely align ourselves to the new realities of today. In order to be truly effective, innovation must be aligned to the direction our world is moving tomorrow (Bishop 2000). Methodologies have been developed to do this efficiently, and today these methodologies are becoming critical business processes to most corporations. It has become a focused practice of many of the world's largest companies. It is a highly researched area through innovation institutes in Ivy League business schools as well as small local colleges.

It takes time to get new strategies moving. If we enact new strategies designed to deal with changes that have *already* happened (*past tense*), we simply align our organizations to the past. See the fundamental flaw? If we align ourselves to the changes happening today, it will take months or years to implement those changes. While hindsight is 20/20, looking backwards will only be of so much help when moving forward down a rapidly winding road. We can no longer survive by aligning ourselves to the past. We have to learn how to align ourselves to the future.

To solve this problem we cannot merely take the current changing conditions we see today and extrapolate them into the future. We can't just look backwards to see what's possible tomorrow. Doing so constrains our thinking. If we simply extrapolated our space program as it was developing in 1961, we would probably have never landed a man on the moon. Kennedy's moon speech set off an incredible decade of innovation, when none of it previously even seemed possible. Likewise, you cannot extrapolate medieval cathedrals out of little country churches. We have to significantly expand our horizons and look beyond ourselves. Extrapolation also fails to work when conditions change rapidly. New trends are emerging on the horizon, producing fast moving waves of change. If we take the time, we can understand how these waves will impact the future; but failing to take these waves into account is a fatal mistake for organizations. I should know.

In the 1990's, I worked for a small consulting company. Our "cutting edge" planning process got us in the door of some pretty impressive aerospace companies. But even our "sophisticated" process failed to seriously analyze new emerging changes and trends. As a result, in one short year, the emerging trends turned into a tsunami of change that swept over the aerospace industry. When it did, it took out one of our biggest clients, one of the largest aerospace contractors. It was absolutely clear: traditional methods of planning for the future were no longer enough for today's world. Change is indiscriminate. It doesn't matter how large you are.

It is becoming increasingly clear: those who align themselves with the future are consistently better prepared. They stay ahead of the curve by having strategies in place by the time the future arrives. It's driven by an insatiable curiosity that seeks to understand the changes happening around us; changes which others miss. (Oster 2011) The more we understand these changes, the better we are at finding creative solutions we can begin implementing today.

More and more businesses are using a certain set of tools to help align their organizations with the future. These tools help leaders make sense of turbulent waters and rapid change. Instead of merely trying to catch up, these tools help you align yourself with the future as it emerges. They help you recognize changes even *before* they emerge. The tools given in this book allow you, the reader, to develop your God-given talent of creativity.

Just as creative artists go to art institutes to learn the science behind color, texture, and layout, there is a science behind the process of innovation. In the coming chapters we will explore some of the greatest forces of change in our world. We will learn why these changes are happening, and how to take advantage of these changes. We will explore how God himself teaches us in the Bible to be researchers of the world in which he's placed us.

We will study a natural process called "creative destruction," which drives the process of creativity and discovery. We will explore how trends interact to create the future. We'll learn to look at the future not as a singular prediction, but as a realm of various possibilities with varying degrees of probability.

This book seeks to explain the scenario planning process used by large corporations and adapt it to ministry and missions. Tangible real-world examples will help us explore the implications of these changes on our people, our organizations and our leaders. Finally, you will be given some best practices to help you get started implementing the new strategies and ideas developed.

CHAPTER 2

MEGA-TRENDS DRIVING CHANGE IN OUR WORLD

"Look at the nations and watch—and be utterly amazed." Habakkuk 1:5

This chapter examines the most significant changes happening in our world today. We call these changes "mega-trends" because they have a nearly universal impact. Governments, businesses, retailers, and secular non-profits study these mega-trends because the future of their organizations depends upon it. Our goal in studying these is to create sustainable, transformational ministry impact with continued impact even as these changes occur around us (Bishop 2000). Understanding where these trends are moving helps us understand the emerging future, before it arrives.

There are significant ways to study the future (Schultz 2002). Trends, events, issues, choices, and cultural aspirations are all powerful influences that are shaping the future (Bishop 2000; Polk 1973). Identifying change as it happens allows us to prepare and to have a greater impact (Bishop 2000). Instead of merely reacting, we become proactive, influencing and shaping changes as they emerge.

Eight mega-trends are listed, six in this chapter dealing with the world in general, and two more in the next chapter regarding changes within global Christianity. Each trend explores changes, many of which aren't yet fully developed, but could grow into movements, producing a dramatically different future than we anticipate (Gladwell 2000).

Each mega-trend will have positive and negative aspects. The goal is not to evaluate whether trends are good or bad. The goal is to identify what is happening, and track the potential future impact (Cornish 2004). Later, we can contemplate our specific response to each trend; should we attempt to influence the trend as it develops, or do we need to adjust our broader strategies?

This list is by no means exhaustive. Different researchers have different methods of classifying these changes. To further spark your own creative thinking, check the references for other books and authors, and their perspectives.

GLOBALIZATION

Globalization is our first mega-trend. The Merriam-Webster dictionary defines globalization as "the development of an increasingly integrated global economy marked especially by free trade, free flow of capital, and the tapping of cheaper foreign labor markets" (Merriam-Webster Dictionary 2013). For our purposes, we will focus on globalization as the integration of world resources and its resulting impact on world mission. This integration of world resources is interconnecting our world in an ever-increasing pace (Friedman 2005). For instance, it is now commonplace for companies to have virtual global teams, whose multinational members are geographically dispersed across the globe (Cummings and Worley 2008). This multicultural diversity is creating a host of new creative ideas and opportunities, partly because of the greatly expanded diversity of backgrounds and experiences of the team members.

The interconnection of global resources is creating tremendous benefits for many. Yet it also creates a whole new set of challenges (Daft 2008). Pittsburgh was once called the Steel City, but today, you'd be hard pressed to find any steel mills there. Today, iron ore is shipped from Brazil to Korea where it is made into steel. That steel is then shipped to the United States at a price much cheaper than what's able to be manufactured locally. Because of globalization, products that use steel are dramatically cheaper, ultimately benefiting the vast majority of American consumers. The economies of Brazil and Korea have also benefited in tremendous ways. The challenge came as a host of Pittsburgh steelworkers refused to be retrained for new jobs in other industries. Decades later, many blindly wait for the steel industry to return. Pittsburgh's new economy is built upon new industries, including technology and health care. For those willing to change, there are tremendous new opportunities.

Globalization fundamentally changes the way remote peoples think and interact with their world (Friedman 2005). For instance, a Bangladesh village recently won an international sustainable enterprise award from the British Council (British Council 2013). The village has significantly reduced poverty as its women make high-end women's handbags, which are sold on the global market through the Internet. Globalization has leveled out the playing field to the point that remote villages in the developing world are able to compete with companies like Gucci and Prada.

In the business world, globalization has led to the idea of outsourcing. Outsourcing is the process of moving tasks from a central location and into the global economy. Work is sent to be completed in the places with the best talent at the best cost. My friend's programming company, for instance, was started almost entirely with Pakistani programmers. This type of outsourcing is seen as manufacturing, computer programming, data processing and phone centers, etc. are moved out to the utter most parts of the earth. Now, even American lawyers are outsourcing legal research and brief writing to other countries, such as India (Economist 2010).

Companies track the strengths and weaknesses of various global economies, in order to know the best location to place a call-center, programming department, manufacturing plant, design team, etc. Yet, few mission organizations have taken advantage of this outsourcing movement. One Bible translation ministry, however, is now outsourcing its translation process in hopes of completing the task of having a Bible in all 6,900 languages by the end of 2025 (Draper 2010). They are creating a software platform where communities translate the Bible online together in a process called "crowd-sourcing" (Wycliffe 2012). Moderators rate the translation ability of each individual and more difficult sections are given to the better translators. The software also helps ensure terms are translated consistently by all translators. This ministry could have chosen to protect its translation process by restricting it to its professional, highly trained translators. Instead, they are opening up the work to managed crowds, who they've found can produce dramatically faster results which are often times as good as, and sometimes better, than their own highly trained scholars.

As with outsourcing, another US-based mission organization is finding increased success by partnering with emerging global mission movements from other parts of the world. The organization was using American missionaries to teach East Asian pastors about church planting and disciple making movements. Yet after the training, few chose to implement any of the concepts. In an attempt to solve this problem, the organization looked to globalization. They invited pastors from India who had started church planting movements themselves to come and perform the training on their behalf (businesses would have labeled this as "outsourcing"). While the training was almost identical, the East Asian pastors indicated feeling a deeper connection with the Indian pastors due to common ground. The East Asians also indicated a higher ability to implement more of what they learned, and a few potential movements are starting to emerge. Provided we don't become protectionist, globalization provides a host of opportunities to partner in new ways, where everyone benefits.

Globalization is also changing the social problems we face. Prostitution rings are now global in nature. According to the U.S Department of Health and Human Services, as many as 800,000 women are trafficked across international borders each year, half of which are under eighteen years old (US Dept. of Health and Human Services 2007). It is estimated that 17,500 of those trafficked women were taken into the United States to work in forced sex labor.

International human trafficking is much broader than the exploitation of women (or men). In the United States, international labor trafficking is an increasing problem.US Health and Human services is struggling to combat a growing sophisticated international network for obtaining, harboring, and transporting men and women to work in the agriculture, manufacturing, construction, domestic work, restaurant, janitorial, and other industries. HHS says the tools of this modern day form of slavery are fraud, coercion, debt bondage, etc.

The globalization of crime isn't just limited to the trafficking. The National Geographic Channel's program "Drugs, Inc." discusses how a Mexican drug cartel sells marijuana grown in Colorado, on the streets of Seattle. Legalized marijuana from Colorado is a higher potency than that which is grown in Central America. As a result, the cartels are reversing the direction of the trafficking; America is becoming producer, and the cartels are bringing it South. Other news shows a potential connection between the Chinese mafia and the murder of a family in Albany, New York (Grondahl 2014). Social problems are increasingly global in nature.

Globalization causes small changes in one place to create ripple effects in unexpected places thousands of miles away. The full effects of globalization are widespread and too numerous to detail. This list here was merely to get you started thinking about Globalization. Globalization is also closely tied to our next mega-trend.

TECHNOLOGY

The technology mega-trend includes all changes related to "computers, medicine, transportation, and other technologies" (Cornish 2009, Kindle location 523). Technology is not just changing the way we communicate with others, it is changing the way we think (Greenfield 2012). It's also changing the way we practice our religious beliefs as well (Fox 2010). Some fear technology; thinking that technological advances like robotics ultimately decrease the number of jobs available. Yet, it has been clearly shown that technological advance creates many more jobs than it destroys (Tansey, Darnton, & Wateridge 2003). These new jobs, however, often require new training. This spells opportunity for those willing to change.

The effects of technology are reaching further than ever before. Just a few years ago, few Chinese had access to an Internet connection; yet by 2014, more half of China's population was online (CNNIC 2013). It is interesting to note, however, that their primary method of getting online is not through a PC. It's through low cost smart phones. In 2012, the cheapest Chinese Android smartphone was fifty dollars (Esteve 2013). In 2014, that same phone costs less than thirty dollars. This dramatic decrease in the cost to get online has transformed even the most remote of villages.

The global changes in technology were made vivide as I recently walked through a village in Northern Thailand, on border of Laos. I was traveling with an American nurse who lived in that village. As we stopped to eat, a villager ran to meet with us, saying, "I saw on Facebook that there was an American who lived in our village and spoke our language perfectly. I came to see if it was true!"

Connectivity to handheld devices is fueling an unprecedented change. The Chinese e-book market is exploding (Kopp 2013). Low cost smartphones permeate Asia; even for the poor. Subway cars and noodle shops are full of young adults voraciously reading e-books. We may not be far from a tipping point in China from print to electronic books. What are the implications for Christian publishing? What might be the effect on the ability to censor public thought? Are we prepared?

Locals often embrace technology much faster than missionaries (Seipp 2013). Cambodian Christians share MP3 Bible stories between cell phones via Bluetooth connections. In America researchers count household computer ownership to gauge technological impact, yet in the developing world, if just one farmer in a village of one hundred buys a computer and gets online, the entire village is transformed. Chinese farmers gather for their worship services around a computer screen. They sing to downloaded Chinese MP3 worship songs while reading the words on downloaded PowerPoint presentations.

Use of technology among national pastors is often split along generational lines. The old reject technology while the young embrace it. One group holds the present while the other holds the future. How do we bridge the gap? How do we respond? Do our future missions teams need to employ programmers who will distribute e-books and develop mobile applications for training, discipleship, etc?

It's not just about phones. In developing countries, the technology of widespread immunizations and rural medicine has dramatically reduced infant mortality while concurrently extending the lives of the elderly (HRSA 2013; Cornish 2004). These positive changes create a host of new problems. The number of retired people is growing faster than their economies and social security systems can adapt (Cornish 2004). Poverty levels are increasing among the elderly. Medicine has extended lives past the point that families were traditionally able to provide care in the home. Most societies around the world are not ready for these changes. Who will house, feed and care for these elderly? The protestant missionary force started with an emphasis on creating schools and universities; its next contribution may be made in building nursing and elder care facilities.

Technology is opening up tremendous new opportunities. Missionaries in remote areas of Uganda and Honduras are distributing Kindle reading devices filled with Bibles and open source seminary materials (Henderson 2013). Likewise, Kindles are also being used in Cuba and India to bring seminary education to thousands of emerging pastors where Internet access isn't available. Another innovative mission organization is creating a mobile seminary in a wallet sized device. Instead of trying to solve the Internet connectivity problem, this device brings the online seminary to them. Classes, lectures, and even tests are brought to the students through this self-contained seminary "hotspot." Since the Internet isn't available, content isn't uploaded or downloaded; instead, memory cards containing content and test scores are mailed back and forth through the postal system.

Bitcoin was created in 2009, and within just a couple of years it had already made a significant world-wide impact. Police, ministries, and prevention organizations will all have to adapt. Other digital currencies are being created too. There is much more opportunity for even greater changes to happen in the future.

Other transformational technologies are emerging as well. 3D printing is revolutionizing a host of industries, as low cost printers can create objects out of an increasing number of materials. We are not far from the time when artificial limbs, dentures, and a host of other medical devices can be printed onsite in remote areas.

Other technologies seek to harness the power of the vast numbers of people online. Crowd funding is changing the way small businesses get started. Some are trying crowd funding as a source for mission funding and even for BAM activities. We've already mentioned the idea of crowd based Bible translation.

New technologies are being created faster than the trends can be tracked, and it is revolutionizing our world in the process.

ECONOMIC CHANGE

As mentioned above, globalization and technology have brought the ability for even the smallest remote villages to participate in the international playing field. In the process, wealth is being created on a level never seen before. The World Bank reports that job creation from China's recent economic growth has brought 600 million Chinese out of poverty from 1981 to 2004 (World Bank 2010). The World Bank credits China as having the greatest and most successful poverty reduction plan the world has ever known. Those involved in Business as Mission may want to take note.

Worldwide, rapid economic development is creating an unprecedented move of people from rural communities into mega-cities. Continuing its growth model, China plans to move a half billion people into its cities by the year 2020 (People's Daily 2003). This urban migration brings a number of new issues which will need to be resolved. Rural poverty and urban poverty are completely different problems, with equally different solutions. In addition, urbanization creates significant strains on water sources, air quality, wildlife, and food supply. As cities grow, these countries rapidly modernize food production creating significant safety concerns. Countless other issues emerge as well (Nsiah-Gyabaah 2012). In the past, many ministries have been concerned with digging wells in the countryside, how could/should ministries respond when the greatest need for clean water is in megacities?

Economic development creates a self-sustaining cycle (Cornish 2004). Development pays for new bridges, roads and other infrastructure which, in turn, facilitate more efficient economic growth. Yet, poverty is still far from being eliminated. In 2013, the United Kingdom saw the greatest drop in family disposable income in twenty-five years (Bingham 2013). America and the UK are experiencing significant economic changes which are squeezing the middle class (Ramesh 2011; US Census Bureau 2013). How will this affect charitable giving? How will this affect the flow of kingdom development resources? How do we prepare for such changes?

These economic changes have a direct impact on projects and missionaries. Future missionaries may find themselves raising their support internationally.

Global partnership opens up a new world of opportunity. One American reports going through missionary training in Seoul, in a Korean church. He now gains a significant part of his support from Koreans. We already mentioned that the next generation of missionaries will be increasingly non-Western. Could it be that the next generation of mission giving will also be non-Western?

We assume kingdom resources must come from the West, but tremendous wealth is being generated in cities like Sao Paulo, Tokyo, Hong Kong, Mexico City, Singapore and Buenos Ares. What if World Vision's next expansion was funded by the Brazilians? Could new seminaries in Senegal be organized by Indians but funded by Singaporeans? What is our responsibility in facilitating the next wave of global Christian resources?

Despite the dramatic advances of other countries, Western ascendency still affects much of our thought. As Westerners, we incorrectly believe that we hold answers to the world's problems (and the resources needed to fuel those answers). Dr. Gupta of the Hindustan Bible Institute in Chennai believes such thinking is a modern form of colonialism. As other economies rise up, non-Western ideas are going to emerge, and many of these ideas may hold better approaches than our own.

The mega-trend of economic change also covers vast changes in the rise and fall of economic powers. Recent changes in pumping levels within OPEC nations have brought rapid changes to the price of oil. This, however, is causing them to spend their national reserves at a tremendous rate. Government subsidies are ending for a long list of items in these countries. There are bound to be ripple effects throughout the region, as well as the world.

Economic changes in Africa are also important to follow. Africa largely missed its own industrial revolution and as a result, is severely lacking in infrastructure. China, however, in a bid to lock in access to sorely needed natural resources, is busy building roads and even stadiums throughout the continent. Increased economic development within Africa will bring increased mobility to its people, both in the region as well as internationally.

The church is the global body of Christ. Increasingly, answers will emerge from some of the most unlikely places. Our global strategies should reflect global realities. Understanding the economics of our global world allows us to think differently about our resources.

DECULTURATION AND RECULTURATION

Deculturation, our fourth mega-trend, is the process of losing one's native culture (Cornish 2004). It's happening worldwide on an unprecedented scale. As people move to cities, and meet other people from cultures different from their own, get connected online, read a wider variety of books, and travel more broadly, they find their traditional language and customs have less importance in their lives. People begin conforming to a diverse combination of cultural norms from the new people they meet in a process of reculturation. They lose their own native culture, and gain something else.

The speed of this process is often increased through government programs designed to integrate minority groups into the cultural mainstream (Yi 2008). One ripple effect is that the total number of world languages is expected to be cut in half, from 6,000 to 3,000 (Cornish 2004). How will this impact mission strategy? How will it impact translation programs?

Because of increased migration to more areas, deculturation is happening faster than ever before. For the most part, people aren't moving into communities with others from their old hometown as they did in the past. Instead, they are finding themselves working and living alongside individuals from a variety of different cultures. Both the city and the individual are transformed by the multitude of cultures interacting (Plaut, Markus, Treadway, and Fu 2012). Values, norms, and ethics are continuously evolving as diverse people interact (Polak 1973).

One might expect a singular, world-wide super-culture to emerge. Yet, this is not what we observe. The emerging culture in Shanghai is significantly different than the emerging cultures of Johannesburg, Rio, New Delhi, and Singapore. While some cultures die out through deculturation, we are also seeing the birth of entirely new cultures through reculturation. The more people interact, the faster the process occurs.

Each new culture is uniquely driven by the society's ideals and images of the future (Polak 1973). Because each city represents a unique collection of various tribes and peoples, each with its own ideals and images, the emerging cultures of these cities are equally unique. These cultural images can change over time. Images of the future are powerful forces, and they often become self-fulfilling prophesies.

The effects of deculturation are much more complex than explained here. But as with other mega-trends, these changes should provoke our curiosity, causing us to ask new questions: should deculturation and the loss of native languages affect scripture translation priorities? Where will unreached people groups be living ten years from now? How will deculturation change the felt needs of various peoples as they process through change?

MOBILITY

Mobility is another mega-trend. "People, goods, and information move from place to place faster and in greater quantity than ever before . . . Containerization, supertankers, and mechanized port facilities now convey petroleum, automobiles, and other goods around the world at relatively low cost (Cornish 2009, Kindle Location 561)." More than ever people are vacationing internationally, so much so that the vacation industry will likely become the largest industry of the twenty-first century (Cornish 2009, Kindle Location 561). Mobility is also affecting business. Merchants in developing countries are losing ground to international brands which are increasingly mobile, such as Walmart.

We are currently in the midst of the greatest human migration in the history of the world (Hudson 2007). People are moving to cities from their poor agricultural villages at an increasing rate. Low cost transportation allows poor people to seek work in cities that are far from their homes, and far from their native culture as well.

Mobility affects more than people and transportation systems. Disease is becoming increasingly mobile as well, as was evidenced in 2003 with the global impact of the SARS virus (Cornish 2009). Within a few short weeks, one regional outbreak became a worldwide concern. Mobility is also one of the reasons the Zika virus spread even more explosively than SARS, in 2016 (Beaubien 2016).

Information is becoming increasingly mobile through the Internet. Instant translation tools like Skype Instant Translate speeds up this process. With tools from Google and Microsoft, a Ukrainian can easily read news from practically any news site in any language. Some of the translations aren't very good right now, but they are improving at an amazing rate. Facebook plans to make information ubiquitous, by deploying satellites to provide internet access to even the remotest parts of Africa and the world (Lee 2015).

Books are increasingly mobile as well. I personally witnessed the popularity of *The Purpose Driven Life* (Warren 2002) sweep across several Asian countries as it was translated into a host of different languages. All types of information is being disseminated faster than ever before (Cornish 2004).

Mobility radically impacts ministry too. People travel further and further from their community to attend a church that suits them. Community is no longer defined by neighborhoods, but by interests. Family and friendship ties are weakened as people move more often, and become accustomed to transient relationships (Cornish 2004). This further weakens the ties people have to their community and church groups as well. Around the world, community is less and less defined geographically and more and more defined by interests.

Information mobility facilitates the creation of multi-site churches: "one church in many locations." (Surrat, Ligon, and Bird 2006) Many of these churches have one speaker who preaches to thousands of people in multiple locations through satellite or high speed Internet links. As of 2006, 1,500 churches had already become multisite churches. A 2008 article in the *Wall Street Journal,* titled "Inspired by Starbucks: Charismatic Pastors Grow New Flocks Overseas, Using Satellites, DVDs and Franchise Marketing to Spread their Own Brand of Religion"(Alter 2008) highlighted seven multi-site churches which now have international locations.

Mobility has other profound effects as well. Examining the website peoplegroups.org, one can find many of the world's unengaged, unreached people groups living in Europe and the Americas. Some of these migrate for economic reasons, others come as refugees.

Mobility also has a darker side as well. As discussed in globalization above, human trafficking is more of an issue than ever. People are smuggled all over the world, especially to the United States, for cheap labor (Polaris Project 2014). Many local governments, familiar with dealing with local problems, are not prepared for these changes. These issues are exacerbated when considering other mobility issues such as terrorism.

How will mobility impact a focus on people groups when young people move from their remote villages to mega-cities in search of work? How could Christian professionals taking jobs in Muslim cities like Abu Dhabi provide the gospel for unreached people groups? How will mobility impact the growth of the South American mission movement?

ENVIRONMENTAL CHANGE

Pittsburgh is one of the greatest success stories in environmental rebound (Cornish 2004). It once burned so much coal that streetlights stayed on at noon; one executive I knew brought an extra white shirt to work because their first shirt would be gray by lunchtime. Yet today, Pittsburgh has won the award for America's most livable city multiple times in a row (Kalson 2010). This success story is not the norm for much of the developing world. Outside of the West, the world is seeing a significant environmental decline (Cornish 2004).

The United Nations shows there were twenty-three megacities with over 10 million people in 2011; they forecast this number to grow to thirty-seven cities by 2025 (United Nations Department of Economic and Social Affairs 2011). By that time, half the world's population will live in cities of over one million people. All this puts tremendous pressure on the environment, and the effects are far reaching. Asthma, for instance, is becoming a tremendous problem in developing regions (Al-Hajjaj, 2008).

Environmental degradation is negatively impacting food safety in much of the world (WHO 2013). The New York Times' Food Safety page lists a number of our world's growing problems: chemically contaminated milk in New Zealand, up to 90 percent of Chinese rice is contaminated with cadmium, and radioactive spinach in Japan. These barely scratch the surface of the problems (New York Times 2013). The *African Journal of Food, Agriculture, Nutrition and Development* lists aflatoxin food contamination as a persistent problem (Amoako-Attah 2011). The *China Daily* reports that food safety is the Chinese consumer's number one concern (Wang 2013). With globalization, these issues find their way into the global food supply. These contaminated foods are finding their way into western countries. Meats and grains grown in the West or other countries, may be sent to Asia for packaging, then sent back to the West. Investigators are increasingly finding that tracking down the ultimate source of food contamination is simply impossible (*New York Times* 2013).

The growth of these mega-cities is creating an unprecedented strain on water supplies (Marion 2013). Water shortages are having a multiplicative effect. For instance, water used by mega-cities in one country significantly decreases the amount of water received downstream by neighboring countries. With decreased water supplies, these other countries have difficulty irrigating their crops and feeding their own people. Over-use of water also causes desertification, leading to a loss of arable land and further decreasing the food supply. It creates dust storms which increases asthma and other diseases. Desertification is a significant crisis now affecting over 168 countries (Cornish 2004; UNCCD 2013). Water.org reports that contaminated water causes a child's death every 21 seconds, for a total of 3.4 million child deaths each year.

Pollution in China is spiraling out of control. Healthy air shouldn't contain particulate matter above 100 parts per million (ppm) at the 2.5 micron level (United States Environmental Protection Agency 2014). When pollution was just beginning to be a problem, Beijing once cancelled school sports activities when pollution reached 240 (USA Today 2011), yet in 2013, Beijing's Air quality hit 750. The United States Embassy rates over 65 percent of Beijing's days from unhealthy to outright hazardous (Wall Street Journal 2014). In 2015, buildings disappeared in Shenyang as levels topped 1400 ppm, fifty times what the World Health Organization considers safe (BBC 2015). China is not alone in these struggles. Even though China gets most of the press, Forbes reports that India's air quality is 50 percent worse on average (Sola, 2015).

The church has been instrumental in drilling many wells to provide clean water for remote villages. How will our social justice adapt when those villagers have moved to the cities and are equally unable to gain access to clean water? When will access to clean air become just as significant an issue as access to clean water? What social ministries will be needed in such extreme environments?

Missionaries are affected too. In addition to cultural stress and ministry responsibilities, missionaries must deal with these harsh realities. In some areas, missionaries are sent knowing the dangers of crime and the difficulties of obtaining familiar ingredients for cooking. Are they prepared for the dangers from potentially harmful foods or respiratory illness? How does all this relate to the concept of creation care? How should the global church respond if the major issues of our world are increasingly environmental in nature?

This chapter has explored just a few of the major trends impacting our world. These mega-trends are likely to have significant impact on all areas of life. Business and industry study these mega-trends to devise opportunities and new products. Yet these trends will have no less impact on the church and global mission. Each mega-trend offers new opportunities as well as new challenges. In the next chapter, we will examine the mega-trends relating to the Western church, the global church, and the global mission enterprise.

CHAPTER 3

MEGA-TRENDS IN GLOBAL CHRISTIANITY

"I am about to do something new. See, I have already begun!
Do you not see it?" Isaiah 43:19 (NLT)

THE GLOBAL CHURCH, A NEW REALITY

The history of modern mission has been characterized by a series of overlapping eras, each defined by its own particular issues, needs, and approaches. A Baptist named William Carey began the modern era of missions in the year 1772. He popularized the fledgling Protestant mission movement through a pamphlet entitled, "An Enquiry into the Obligations of Christians to Use Means for the Conversion of the Heathens" (Winter and Hawthorne 1999)." In just twenty-five years, over a dozen new mission agencies formed. This first era, predominately driven by European churches, focused on taking the gospel to the coastlands of distant countries. It was primarily characterized by denominational agencies using geographically-based strategies. The era lasted approximately 120 years.

Major Eras of World Mission

The second era of modern mission began in 1865 as Hudson Taylor took an innovative approach to finishing the task by bringing the gospel to the interior regions, far from the coastlands. This era began as the first era was drawing to a close, creating an overlap of about forty-five years. It was characterized by independent mission agencies, and a geographic strategy predominately led by American churches. This era lasted approximately 110 years and ended with the Lausanne Conference of 1974.

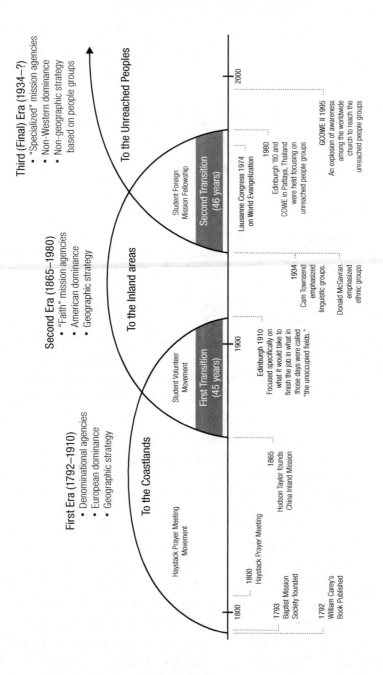

Winter and Hawthorne, *Perspectives on the World Christian Movement*, 1999, 259.

The third (and current) era of modern mission began as the second era drew to a close, in 1934, when Townsend and McGavran devised a new focus based upon ethno-linguistic groups. This era is characterized by specialized agencies focusing on specific services such as medical relief, evangelism, church planting movements, etc. This era is also noted for the entry of non-western churches into the world mission movement.

Perhaps the most significant event of this era was the Lausanne Conference of 1974 (Lausanne Movement 2013). This historic meeting brought about a unified focus on evangelism and discipleship. The conference was an outgrowth of Billy Graham and Christianity Today's Conference on World Evangelism held in Berlin, 1966. This was soon followed by other conferences in Singapore, the United States, and Australia. Billy Graham, however, felt the need for a larger conference which would unify evangelicals for the purpose of finishing the task. Over 2700 individuals from 150 nations converged in Lausanne, Switzerland. Ralph Winter gave the plenary address, "The Highest Priority, Cross Cultural Evangelism," which focused on unreached people groups, and has since been seen as a turning point for the most recent era.

Dr. John Stott and Billy Graham spoke to the need to approach ministry not as colonialist outsiders, but as servants to the national peoples. Dr. Francis Schaeffer spoke to the fact that the process of evangelism is much wider than simply sharing the good news. At the time, many "evangelism movements" were taking entire countries by storm. Yet, the Lausanne working groups brought an understanding that the gospel was more than proclamation (evangelization) of the Word alone. Jesus' command was that people be discipled to obey everything Jesus taught. Evangelism movements were found to be far short of this command. They focused on telling. Discipleship, however, requires people to slow down and ask questions, taking all the time necessary to help people where they are, to obey Christ.

The next significant change from Lausanne came in uniting factions of Christianity focusing either on social justice (compassion ministries) or evangelism. Some Christians were criticized for having a myopic focus on evangelism while others focused on social justice apart from the gospel message. Lausanne brought the two sides of the debate together to discuss the issue of true transformation. Lausanne helped both sides move towards a holistic missiology which seeks individual and social transformation.

Even though 150 nations were represented, Billy Graham criticized the Lausanne conference participants: 85 percent were Western expatriate missionaries while only 15 percent represented national pastors. Graham sent the delegates to back to their respective countries, to stop acting as colonialists, and start being servants. He challenged them to empower the locals through instilling vision and helping them take up the task of evangelizing their own peoples. The focus needed to move towards national churches finishing the task and foreign missionaries working with them in partnership.

Another important outcome was the popularization of church-planting movements (CPM) (Alliance SCP 2008). The Lausanne covenant says that the whole church must take the whole gospel to the whole world; God created his church to finish this task. But, Lausanne highlighted two dangers: churches which solely grow in numbers and, alternatively, churches which solely grow in depth. Healthy churches grow concurrently in both numbers and depth.

Half a century before, Roland Allen had written about the "Spontaneous Expansion of the Church: And the Causes that Hinder It," describing the rapid reproduction of churches he observed in China and Africa (1927). Since that time, more and more missionaries have taken note of similar movements happening naturally around the world. Billy Graham's insistence at Lausanne that the task be completed by the year 2000, and that it be completed through the empowerment of natives, only fueled the focus on multiplicative church planting and discipleship methods.

The Lausanne covenant states:

> The dominant role of Western missions is fast disappearing. God is raising up from the younger churches a great new resource for world evangelization, and is thus demonstrating that the responsibility to evangelise [sic] belongs to the whole body of Christ. All churches should therefore be asking God and themselves what they should be doing both to reach their own area and to send missionaries to other parts of the world. A reevaluation of our missionary responsibility and role should be continuous. Thus a growing partnership of churches will develop and the universal character of Christ's church will be more clearly exhibited. We also thank God for agencies which labor in Bible translation, theological education, the mass media, Christian literature, evangelism, missions, church renewal and other specialist fields. They too should engage in constant self-examination to evaluate their effectiveness as part of the church's mission. (Lausanne Movement, 2013)

The beginning phrase, "the dominant role of western missions is fast disappearing" is an important concept. It reflects the fact that globalization has moved the center of Christianity away from the West and into the global South and East (Jenkins 2002). For centuries, a majority of Christians were either European or American. Now, the majority of the world's Christians now live in South America, Africa and Asia. This has changed the Christian demographic of the "average Christian" dramatically. Christians in the global South and East are much poorer than their American brothers and sisters (Magee 2013). Today, North America still holds much of Christianity's financial and published resources and much of this literature and theology was developed upon Western Enlightenment thought and linear logic (McGrath 2002). Non-Western Christians often find these writings difficult to understand. The Renaissance and Enlightenment were Western developments which shaped Western thinking and culture. The global South and East went through their own unique development periods, uniquely shaping their cultures and thought processes in ways very different than that of the West.

As the a majority of the world's Christians now live outside of the "West," the global South and East are becoming known as the "majority world." It is interesting to note that entirely new mission movements are emerging from this "majority world." Missions has truly become everywhere to everywhere (Shaw & Wan 2004).

Korea, Brazil, and Nigeria are the fastest growing mission senders. (Magee 2013; Hickman 2013; *Operation World* 2013) Korea is sending twenty thousand missionaries and is growing at a staggering 17 percent. This means Korea is doubling its mission force every 4.1 years. Brazil is currently sending twelve thousand missionaries, and with a 10 percent growth rate, they'll double in just seven years. Nigeria currently sends five thousand missionaries, and is growing at 12 percent per year (Magee 2013; Hickman 2013; *Operation World* 2013). This growth is expected to continue for the long term. Such dramatic increases in non-Western missionaries will lead to profound changes on the ground, in the mission field.

Even though the global church is sending increasing numbers of missionaries, they need significant help to developing their movements. Research shows that most of these movements rarely move beyond the diaspora peoples of their own culture (Center for the Study of Global Christianity 2013). For instance, Chinese missionaries, although going to the Middle East to reach local peoples, generally only reach other Chinese migrant workers working there. The same scenario has been seen for South American missionaries working in Africa. For these growing movements to be effective, the focus must be on equipping these missionaries with the tools for effective cross-cultural ministry.

Such trends should spark our insatiable curiosity to ask new questions, such as: What happens when an American missionary finds themselves working alongside Nigerian missionaries? How will Nigeria's unique church strategies and their theological perspective impact the world mission movement? How can the Western church better appreciate and support Nigeria's unique perspective and contribution? Are there ways we can help Nigeria make a maximum impact?

Jenkins points out that the South and East have a need for new theological works, written by Asians, Africans and South Americans, based upon their own logic and thought patterns (Jenkins 2002). Western Christians will likely find them difficult to understand and accept. The missiology held by the West, is not necessarily the same missiology held by the "majority world." God placed unique traits in the churches of each of these countries, traits that will be brought with them in the same distant lands to which Western missionaries are going.

As stated in the Lausanne Covenant, the Western church cannot continue to act as if the West is the center of Christian thought, theology, mission strategy, etc. (McGrath 2002). It must move from a perspective of ascendency to that of equal partners, even servants, to the rest of the world. Missions is no longer about "the West to the rest" but "everywhere to everywhere" (Shaw and Wan 2004, 16). Western missionaries working in Tanzania may find it difficult when they encounter Brazilian, Korean, and Nigerian missionaries all working with the same people group, but using very different strategies, based on very different values. How will all these groups work together?

The Lausanne covenant shows the need for Western mission agencies to change. This profound statement was penned almost forty years ago, yet, it appears that many mission agencies haven't fully realized just how important this statement is to the current mission environment. The covenant calls for continuous self-examination, and reevaluation of effectiveness within the mission industry. If the role of the West was "fast disappearing" forty years ago, the changes in the world mission movement today should be staggering. Do our own strategies reflect these realities?

This cannot be overstated: the global body of Christ is far different than it was just a few years ago. Today, for the first time in history, a mature church now exists in practically every province of every country of the world (Magee 2013). These are not just immature church plants, but mature churches. This should radically change our perspective. Yet, many of the strategies employed by Western agencies appear to be pre-Lausanne in their thinking. Borthwick recalls one plea from the leader reflecting this reality:

Please send us your adults, and not just your children. I realize that most career missionaries had a short-term experience that played a significant role in determining their future ministry—but I am troubled at the number of children you send our way for one- and two-week trips . . . Please send us some people ready to learn our language and our culture, who can then live and work with us to help us educate and develop our church. Related to this—we really don't need construction workers from your region as we have manual laborers of our own—nor do we need skits and songs in languages we don't understand and music we find interesting but foreign. (Borthwick 2012, 207)

While these words do not necessarily represent the attitude of every national church, they should cause us to take a step back and think about how we engage with majority world churches. The needs of mature churches are significantly different than those of infant church plants or pioneering outreaches. These churches desire assistance from experienced ministry professionals. Yet America continues to primarily push missionaries with little or no professional ministry experience out onto the mission field (Borthwick 2012).

Imagine someone from Ecuador, with a seminary degree but without ministry experience in his own country, arriving at your church's doorstep. In broken English, he says he's come to help your church become more effective. Now imagine someone doing this with little or no training at all. Do we recognize the profound disconnect?

Mission Sending

Missionary sending from the United States appears to have crested with about 120,000 missionaries across all denominations. Average growth rate is a paltry 1.2 percent. Yet, when we look at the number of missionaries sent per million Christians, a different picture emerges. In 1975, the United States sent about 370 missionaries per million Christians. This peaked around the year 2000 with 618 missionaries per million Christians. We have since seen a slight decline to about 614 missionaries sent per million Christians (Magee 2013; Hickman 2013; *Operation World* 2013). The decline may not appear to be significant, but if we plot this data, a traditional S curve pattern emerges (see "S Curves" in Chapter 5). Unless significant changes happen in the United States' mission sending programs, we should expect a steep decline in missionary sending in the near future. Additional data is even more troubling regarding North American mission sending. Short-term missions have long been a driver of long-term mission efforts (Hickman 2013). Research shows that short term Protestant missionary sending (under one year) peaked around 2001 and has since declined by 15 percent. Mid-term missionary sending (1 to 4 years) peaked in 2001 as well and has declined 5 percent. This same data shows that long term Protestant missionary sending likely peaked in 2001 and is now declining by 3 percent. If short-term mission trips drive long-term missionary sending, long term sending should expect a dramatic decline in the near future.

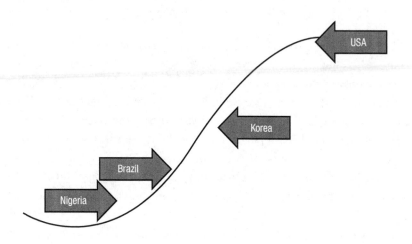

When we first noticed these early indicators of falling missions sending, two years ago, we did not know how true this would prove to be. In February of 2016, David Platt, President of the Southern Baptist's International Mission Board, announced an almost 20 percent reduction in missions staff, an extreme step taken in order to stabilize the agency's finances (Zylstra 2016). This equates to 983 missionaries and 149 other staff positions. The reasons for the decline in missions sending are not entirely known. Some feel that young American Christians don't like the term "missionary," nor do they care for the deputation process (support raising) (Magee 2013). Instead, they choose to live out "missional" lives while applying for foreign expatriate professional jobs overseas (Magee 2013). These jobs give them an income and a chance to develop their skills while they work in the same countries targeted by many mission sending agencies. There, they work in teams with natives in close relationship where they can share their faith. It seems there is a disproportionate number of Christians seeking out these jobs. Maybe this is God's plan; it is forecasted that these same secular expatriate jobs will double between 2016 and 2020 (PWC 2013).

There appears to be a significant contributing factor causing these young Christians to avoid the deputation process. Young graduates (potential missionary candidates) are overburdened with a staggering amount of college debt (Censky 2011). Even those finding secular, high paying jobs are struggling to make ends meet. Expecting these missionary candidates to be debt free is a nearly impossible task. These young believers cringe at the thought of raising funds from the church and their friends to pay off their college debts. For those who still go through with it, raising the additional support to cover the loans feels almost like an impossible task.

These young graduates are different from previous generations in other ways as well. They have a deep desire to form meaningful relationships at work; they have a strong personal and career developmental focus; and they integrate technology into every aspect of their lives (Gyes 2009; Price Waterhouse Coopers 2013). No wonder they seek out these professional jobs, they want to develop themselves as much as possible. Their belief system drives them to integrate their life and ministry together in authenticity (Barna 2011). Social justice is also a significant motivator (Magee 2013).

Research shows that 38 percent of today's college graduates want long-term employment in a job that will proactively teach them new skills with opportunities to be promoted quickly (Gyes 2009). Another 28 percent advance their careers aggressively and will change organizations several times in order to develop a broad experience base. This means a full two-thirds of this generation actively seek companies that will train them up to reach their full potential.

There is another 21 percent that should also be noted. These individuals simply want to find a stable working environment. They express little motivation in their work habits and simply want to collect their paycheck (Gyes 2009). If mission agencies are not intentionally focusing on the developmental needs of the 68 percent likely to be tomorrow's movers and shakers, they risk attracting the 21 percent who are simply seeking stability.

It should be noted that there are several missions agencies which are growing, and growing rapidly. Most of this growth is not due to sending more North Americans; instead, these agencies have "internationalized" their mission force by sending national (non-Western) missionaries (Magee 2013). They are growing because they have chosen to get involved in the global "everywhere to everywhere" mission movement, where God is already moving.

It's important to note that trends don't simply continue on forever; every trend should be watched for signs that change may already be occurring. For instance, researcher Steve Moon believes that South Korean mission sending is much further along than others have anticipated, possibly cresting the upper portion of the growth curve into maturity. He believes the era of fast growth is well behind us. The road ahead for Korean missions, according to Moon, is largely flat; which he ties to the stalling out of the growth of the Korean church in general. This is a great reminder that the reader is encouraged not to simply take and use the information in these mega-trends for making strategies, but to use these mega-trends to help spark new questions, uncover new trends in new areas, and even uncover reversals in previous trends.

Shift from Global North to Global South

As mentioned previously, the global South is rising. South America, Africa, and Asia are seeing rapid conversions to Christianity. These peoples are conservative, poor and generally Pentecostal in nature. (Jenkins, 2002) Just to give an example of how fast Christianity is changing, in 1990, global Christianity was 81 percent white; by 2020, global Christianity will be 70 percent non-white. Christianity is undergoing one of the most massive shifts it has ever known.

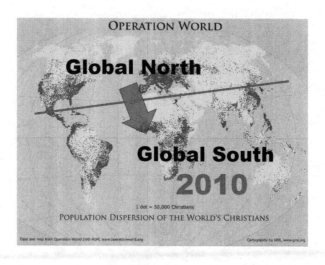

Operation World, 2013

Flow of National Mission Sending

Even though we've been praying for native church movements to emerge, the global North seems to be caught off guard. Eldon Porter, a former executive with SIM states, "We prayed for decades that the Lord would raise up a Latin American missions movement but we never anticipated what the impact of this would be" (Porter 2013). Ultimately, the greatest challenge today's American missions agencies face is maintaining relevancy within this massive shift.

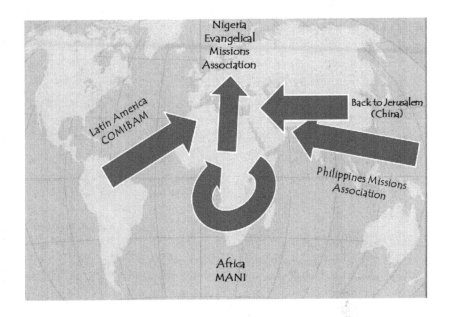

Operation World, 2013

The playing field has changed significantly. Missions agencies face a considerable amount of stress, possibly indicating the beginning of a new, fourth era of world mission. The previous mission eras each lasted about 110–120 years (Winter and Hawthorne 1999). The new eras each began about forty-five years before the old eras ended. Assuming the pattern continues, there should be a thirty-year gap from the end of the last transition period to the beginning of the next transition period. If this holds true, the next era of world mission should have begun around the year 2010.

One writer believes we've already entered this fourth era. The focus, he says, is on the facilitation of national movements. He says the era is categorized by organic, nonhierarchical mission structures with minimal organization. "Only time will tell if we are in another era, or if perhaps this more organic focus is a subset of era 3. Personally, I think that we are moving into something qualitatively different" (Parish 2011, 1).

One thing is for sure, since the last era began, we've seen a mature church emerge in almost every province of every country. This should radically change our game plan. Put this together with the mass migration of unreached and unengaged people groups from rural to urban environments, and we have a completely different chess board (*Operation World* 2013).

It is estimated that 600,000 Chinese now live in France (Laurent 2010). Strategies to reach the all the Burmese used to require a trip to Myanmar. Today such plans must include Burmese refuges living in settlements scattered around the United States. (PA Refugee Resettlement Program 2013) A purely people group focus is becoming an extremely complex endeavor.

THE CHANGING AMERICAN CHURCH

The environment surrounding American churches is also changing dramatically. Some have interpreted these changes as doomsday scenarios foretelling the end of American Christianity (McGrath 2002). Olson's research shows US church attendance at 18 percent and declining quickly (MacDonald 2009). One forecast estimates 20 million will leave the American church by 2020 (Gary 2012). It should be noted that many of these doomsday forecasts are built upon correlations with the decline of the European church and the decline of American denominations (McGrath 2002).

The future of the American church may not be as dark as some foresee. Gallop reports regular church attendance remaining steady at about 40 percent for the last several decades (Newport 2010). Gallop polls also show an increase in the number of people believing that a "born again" experience is necessary for salvation (Winseman 2005). This number has grown from 33 percent in 1983 to 48 percent in 2005. The number of people believing in "essential evangelical beliefs" has held steady for years at 22 percent of the population.

Polls about American society tell us a different story. Society's perceptions of marriage, sex, morality, family, etc. are moving significantly away from a traditional Christian perspective. According to the Barna Research Group, agnostics have risen dramatically from 10 percent in 2011 to 17 percent in 2013 (American Bible Society 2013). CNN stated that Christianity is on its way to becoming a despised American minority (Blake 2013). Whatever you believe about the polls on church attendance, the church appears to be losing the battle for America's majority culture (McGrath 2002).

The way we practice our beliefs is also changing. Multi-site churches (like them theologically or not) appear to be here to stay (Stetzer 2013). The concept has attracted its share of proponents and harsh critics. Ecclesiological debate aside, research shows that multi-site churches baptize more people into Christ and mobilize more people into ministry than single-site churches. Sixty-two of the fastest one hundred growing churches in the United States are multi-site churches. Interestingly, there is no single multi-site model; every multi-site church appears to have a unique strategy. The multi-site movement is a great example of diverse innovation within a common theme.

Research shows that Christians are leaving traditional denominations in favor of non-denominational churches (McGrath 2002). In response, denominational churches are quickly shedding any denominational references in their names, hoping to stem the tide. Church giving is also down significantly with believers giving an average of just 2 percent of their annual income (Ronsvalle and Ronsvalle 2013). Fewer young people are identifying with church denominations and structures, calling them "manmade institutions."

Researchers have found average young American adults are "above all else, idealists who longed for authenticity, and having failed to find it in their churches, they settled for a non-belief that, while less grand in its promises, felt more genuine and attainable" (Taunton 2013, 5). One individual states, "Christianity is something that if you *really* believed it, it would change your life and you would want to change [the lives] of others. I haven't seen too much of that" (Taunton 2013, 5). Not finding this authenticity in the church, they choose non-belief as a more authentic lifestyle.

Cars gave people the ability to drive further distances in search for churches suiting their own needs and beliefs. As such, churches have lost their place as the geographic center of our towns. Attendees no longer come from one or two nearby communities, they now come from a multitude of communities spanning broad regions and cities. As the church found it increasingly difficult to care for the needs of so many communities, it outsourced most of its benevolence to non-profits in order to focus more completely on evangelism and discipleship.

When these churches were the center of a community, "the church was a focal point of philanthropy. Now parachurch ministries, schools, and charitable agencies compete for those dollars" (Ronsvalle 2008). As a result, it is becoming much more difficult to see a church's specific impact on the community in which it is located. Could this change be influencing young people's perceptions that the church is not being authentic in its practices?

Despite the church's focus on discipleship and evangelism, young Christians are passionately driven by social justice issues (Borthwick 2012). Research shows social justice rapidly supplanting evangelization as the main mission driver for the global North. (Magee 2013) Evangelism and church planting is no longer "cool" to younger Christians who desire to see immediate tangible impacts from their efforts. This shift has sparked a tremendous debate within the church regarding its relationship to the gospel. Borthwick states, "Social justice is the main driver of missions moving forward, yet young adults' idea of involvement is going to a social justice conference and making a donation using their parent's credit card. These young adults want to make a difference but don't know how; and they are overburdened with college debt" (Borthwick 2013).

Social justice may be linked to another change. Global North Christians are struggling with pluralistic views to salvation (Borthwick 2012). Simply stated, there's a silent debate as to whether Jesus is the *only* way to heaven. It should come as no surprise that this debate affects a believer's willingness to go to the ends of the earth to make disciples of all peoples. This debate was brought center stage with the publication of Rob Bell's book, *Love Wins* which openly questions the existence of Hell and raises the possibility that all, including non-believers, attain eternal life (Bell 2011).

In the middle of all this is an interesting theological trend called New Calvinism, and it is having a significant impact on the future of North American Christianity (Patton 2010). It is a resurgence of Calvinism, being made popular by preachers such as Mark Driscoll, R.C. Sproul, Tim Keller, and John Piper. The movement reflects a "God-centered reformation" among young adults and is marked by a rejection of church "fluff" (Walker 2010). New Calvinists have an intense desire for devoted study of the scripture. While only 10 percent of current pastors are Calvinist, 30 percent of new seminary graduates are Calvinist, marking a significant and sudden increase, sure to have an impact (Patton 2010). The trend points to the emergence of a strongly devoted generation of young adults who take the word of God seriously in the midst of a highly secularized society. America is polarizing.

According to Gordon Conwell Theological Seminary (Crosby 2012) and Pew Research (LeClaire 2012), the fastest growing component of Christianity is Pentecostalism. Pentecostals make up one fourth of all evangelical Christians and are continuing to grow much faster than any other segment. Much of this growth is connected to strong focus upon church planting. How will the continued growth of these Pentecostal "renewalists" (as Gordon Conwell Theological Seminary refers to them) and New Calvinists impact the future of the world mission movement?

The growth of Islam in America, sometimes called "Islamification," is getting a tremendous amount of press time. Some believe, however, that it is overblown and getting more press than the movement deserves (Newport 2012). The argument is that the more significant impact is the "Hispanification" of America. Of all American immigrants, 53 percent are Hispanic. (Murray 2012) These 14.2 million Hispanic Americans are deeply religious and overwhelmingly Christian. A full 37 of all Latinos identify themselves as Evangelical (including Protestants and Catholics). Many are leaving the Catholic tradition for Protestant Churches. It should be noted that evangelical Hispanics proselytize aggressively. Forecasts expect Hispanics will make up 20 percent of the United States population by the year 2030. This will bolster conservative American values and provide an interesting counterweight against secularization.

COMHINA is an organization mobilizing and equipping American Hispanic churches to evangelize unreached people groups, worldwide. (COMHINA 2014) Hispanics represent a small but growing force in missions, and could also prove to become the next great American mission force. Can existing agencies accommodate a U.S Spanish speaking mission force of cultural Hispanics?

Technology is changing the way Christians live out their faith. Technology made multi-site churches possible. Many churches now display hash tags during sermons to encourage congregants to tweet interactively during the sermon. Seventy percent of millennial Christians read the Bible on a portable device. (Barna 2013) Forty percent now donate electronically. Thirty-eight percent report fact-checking their pastor's sermons as they listen to them preach.

Another significant shift includes refocusing on the Missio Dei:

> During the past half a century or so there has been a subtle but nevertheless decisive shift toward understanding mission as God's mission. During preceding centuries mission was understood in a variety of ways ... Often it was perceived in ecclesiastical categories: as the expansion of the church (or of a specific denomination) ... The classical doctrine on

the missio Dei as God the Father sending the Son, and God the Father and the Son sending the Spirit was expanded to include yet another "movement": The Father, Son, and the Holy Spirit sending the church into the world. As far as missionary thinking was concerned, this linking with the doctrine of the Trinity constituted an important innovation . . . Mission is thereby seen as a movement from God to the world; the church is viewed as an instrument for that mission. There is church because there is mission, not vice versa. To participate in mission is to participate in the movement of God's love toward people. (Bosch 1991)

Because of this shift, mission is no longer just seen as a function of the church. Now more than ever, the church understands that its existence is built upon the mission of God. As a consequence, churches are redefining the "mission field" as the places in which we live and work (Borthwick 2012). There's a greater focus on mission, but foreign mission isn't getting the same publicity as it did before. Foreign mission looks different in these "missional" churches. These churches see the *Missio Dei* as their own church's responsibility often causing them to become directly involved with overseas churches. Traditional mission agencies are bypassed, and the wisdom and experience from a long history of mission involvement is often forgotten. Dr. Jay Gary, one of the lead developers for the class "Perspectives on the World Christian Movement," says "we are in the age of the amateurs" (Gary 2013).

Mission agencies, already hurting from a decrease in North American missionary sending, may find themselves having to justify their role in the emerging paradigm. Some will undoubtedly refuse to change while blaming the challenges on the enemy of the church who is seeking to kill and destroy their plans. While the enemy is at work, he may be getting more credit than he's due. Others will simply recognize that times are changing; the cloud is lifting and moving on, and there's an opportunity to follow the cloud as it leads us upon new pathways.

The changes outlined here barely scratch the surface. I hope you are convinced that the world of missions is changing rapidly and that structures and strategies need to adapt appropriately. Moving forward, we need to continue watching so that we may anticipate the future as it emerges (Oster 2011). We cannot simply align ourselves to the new realities of today; it takes time to implement new strategies, and doing so only orients the future of our organizations to the past. We need to align ourselves to tomorrow.

CHAPTER 4

GOD AND INNOVATION

"Wisdom is supreme—so acquire wisdom, and whatever you acquire, acquire understanding!" Proverbs 4:7 (NET)

INNOVATION AND MINISTRY

When people don't see the results they are accustomed to, they often double down on their existing strategies only to find the old methods no longer work as they once did. Greater and greater effort is expended for fewer and fewer results. Meanwhile, strategic drift widens, decreasing effectiveness (Burke 2011). If God's people recognize that a decrease in effectiveness is due to changes happening in their environment, and they have faith that God wants to help them be more effective, they will have the faith to begin innovating. "Innovation provides . . . the opportunities to grow faster, better, and smarter . . . and ultimately to influence the direction of their industry" (Davila, Epstein, and Shelton 2011). As we've seen, the church is in no way immune to strategic drift. The church was created to perform certain functions (prayer, worship, preaching, discipleship, etc.) but the Bible is largely silent on any specific methods to perform these functions (Alliance SCP 2008). The church must continually adapt to the surrounding culture in order find pathways which will bring the unchanging truths of the Bible into a changing world.

The church is still adapting. Who today regularly uses the 1500's translation of Tyndale's English New Testament, or the 1560 Geneva Bible? When I first became a Christian, I read the Today's English Version for its readability. In the 90's when I studied theology, I used the New American Standard. Different times require different methods and tools. Language is also in a constant state of change. Ever wonder why we see a continuous stream of new revisions and translations? The Bible translators are simply reacting to continuous strategic drift

Worship preferences change too, otherwise pipe organ makers would be fairing much better than they are today. Few today would find themselves drawn to a 1700's Puritan style worship service. Culture changes, and the church adapts (Wolfe 2008). When churches stop adapting to the needs of the community, attendance drops, and they eventually die (Alliance SCP 2008). When churches die, we must be careful not to give the devil too much credit especially if the problem is due to our own inability to recognize and respond to change.

In Europe, when the surrounding culture began to change rapidly, church attendance began to decline (McGrath 2002). Instead of adapting, churches had another way to survive—they were propped up by government assistance. Many of these churches had become government sponsored monopolies. Some pastors were even appointed by the state. Strategies designed to help the church only further insulated it from the cultural changes happening in the community. Then, after the World Wars, the cultural changes gained momentum. British researcher and theologian, McGrath, credits the subsequent demise of Christianity in Europe with a profound disconnect between the pastorate and societal issues (2002). According to McGrath, strategic drift killed the European church, while pastors blamed society's spiritual apathy.

It's interesting to note that McGrath has great hope for the American church. He doesn't expect it will experience the same dramatic decline. As the American church has no artificial external assistance, it has been forced to innovate over and over again in order to maintain membership in a changing world. Since the government isn't there to prop up ineffective churches, new churches continuously fill the gap left by the strategic drift of slower moving churches.

When Paul brought the gospel to the Gentiles, he incorporated innovative new cultural ways of worship and spiritual life (Acts 13). Though his strategies were successful among the Gentiles, his acts were condemned by the apostles who had been closest to Jesus (Acts 15). They called Paul to Jerusalem in an attempt to force him to return to "proper" methodology. Imagine for a moment if Paul had relented. Christianity would likely have remained something akin to a movement within Judaism. World-wide, individuals would have to become cultural Jews upon conversion to Christianity. In such an environment, Rome would likely never have been converted. Ephesus would never have become the center of Christianity for the next 150 years (Siebeck 2004). Praise God that Paul was willing to stand up for innovation in ministry methods, even to the reproach of his peers (Acts 18:6).

Ministry innovation has continued through the centuries. Sub-Saharan African churches worshiping under the largest spreading tree look and feel different from suburban American churches, these look and feel different from Chinese house churches and Greek Orthodox churches. Even in America, worship styles vary extensively among different ethnic groups. Praise God for diversity.

Ministries must continue to innovate as culture changes around them. Those who fail will eventually find themselves becoming irrelevant (Oster 2011). Jack Welch, former CEO of GE Corporation stated, "We've long believed that when the rate of change inside an institution becomes slower than the rate of change outside, the end is in sight. The only question is when."(Hines & Bishop 2006, 178)

A Faith-Based Image of the Future

The way we view the future has incredible implications (Polak 1973). When a society's view of the future shifts dramatically to the negative, the society falls (Miller 2001). On the other hand, when views of the future swing dramatically to the positive, those societies rise. Our thoughts have significant consequences.

God cares about the way we think about the future. In the Bible, God reminds us time after time to have faith. The command to "be strong and courageous" was given to countless people, many of whom faced seemingly insurmountable odds. God said this to Joshua (Deut 31:6), to Hezekiah (2 Chron 32:7–8), to the disciples (Matt 14:27), and even to church of today (1 Cor 16:13). Without faith, it is impossible to please God (Heb 11:6).

God takes a strong interest in our thoughts about the future. Abram had no heir and his wife's body was well beyond the time she should have been able to have children (Gen 15:2, 18:13). Yet God promised that Abram would have off-spring as numerous as the stars (Gen 15:5). Although he had no tangible reason to be positive about the future himself, Abraham believed, and to God, this was righteousness (Gen 15:6).

We cannot underestimate the importance God lays upon the way we choose to see the future. God repeatedly calls upon mankind to trust him for its personal future as well as the future of nations. When people in the Bible respond in faith to God, God raises them to power. Those refusing a faith-based view of the future are brought down. Even when Israel faced seemingly catastrophic challenges (such as being led captive to Babylon), God called them to have faith. He called them to believe that he would prosper them wherever they were (Jer 29). The

Bible presents faith as a present, conscious choice to believe in God's positive intervention in the future.

In faith Peter got out of the boat believing he would walk among the waves and turbulent waters (Matt 14:29–30). Yet, as soon as Peter took his eyes off Christ and saw the waves, his orientation toward the future changed abruptly to the negative. Christ still saved him, but called out his negative perspective: "Why did you doubt?" (Matt 14:31). Faith believes Christ will intersect with our future, changing it for good and not for evil (Jer 29:11).

Societies must maintain a positive view of the future (faith) in order to survive (Polak 1973). Such faith is self-reinforcing, and builds momentum. If secular scientists recognize the need for this kind of faith, how much more should Christians? We have the very Light of the World residing inside of us (Matt 5:14). We have Christ's promise to be with us even to the end of the age (Matt 28:20). Christ has promised to build his church and to partner with us in order to accomplish that end (Matt 16:18). Regardless of our present circumstances, the very gates of hell are powerless against His plans (Matt 16:18).

We already know the outcome of the game, so it doesn't matter if we find ourselves down by seven runs at the bottom of the ninth inning with two outs, no one on base and our worst player is at bat. No matter how steep the odds, we know the outcome. All God's promises are true (2 Cor 1:20).

Our first fundamental step towards innovation is to maintain faith in Christ that he holds the future. We often don't have the answers, and for some reason, it is to God's glory to conceal his plans (Prov 25:2). Since the fall in the Garden, we are no longer able to converse with him face to face , yet, it is a noble undertaking to search out and understand the plans of God (Gen 2, 3; Prov 25:2). For the Christian, innovation is the process of finding out what God is doing to change the future, and joining in with him in those plans (Blackaby 2013).

Christianity is unique when it comes to being innovative (Oster 2011). The Christian God is creative, and since we were created in his image, our innovation becomes, "a form of worship . . . Every person is creative and innovative, because the capacity to be so was designed into us by the God who made us. We innovate because we are made to resemble the Great Innovator" (Oster 2011, Kindle location 70, 562). When we innovate, we glorify God.

Issachar: knowing what's next

We find one of the most notable Biblical stories of innovators in 1 Chronicles 12. Here David, banished from King Saul's presence, is forced to retreat to Ziklag.

There are impressive descriptions of the mighty warriors who come to his aid: some are trained to shoot arrows and use slings with both right and left hands, others are fast as gazelles, and some have faces like lions. The least of the Gadites could hold off a hundred men, and the greatest, a thousand. Such descriptions continue from verse one to fifteen, and again from twenty-three to thirty-seven. In the midst of this impressive list, a group of two hundred men is singled out—but interestingly, not for impressive strength or fighting ability.

The Hebrew states that these two hundred men possessed the ability to discern the times with wisdom and find meaning (Strongs 1995). "From Issachar there were 200 leaders and all their relatives at their command—they understood the times and knew what Israel should do" (1 Chron 12:32; NET). That all two hundred of these leaders were trained as innovative thinkers was of particular interest to the writer of 1 Chronicles. They found it worthy of recording for the ages, just as worthy as someone who could fight like a lion or wield a sword with both hands.

Today's organizations might employ a handful of people who dedicate a portion of their time to be strategic planners, helping the organization stay the course. Yet, this tribe of Issachar was different. All two hundred were trained in the skills necessary to recognize and understand changes happening around them. More importantly, they were innovators, understanding how to position themselves favorably within those changes. They created a culture of strategic, innovative thinking, and this ability made them into mighty warriors. All two hundred leaders were trained innovative leaders.

If the tribe of Issachar could do this three thousand years ago, there is no reason we cannot do it today. As we look at the challenges of today's climate, imagine the power of creating an organization of innovators. This concept is being rediscovered in modern business (Porras and Silvers 1991). In order to keep up with the rapid changes, secular businesses are finding that it isn't enough to have one transformational idea. Today's businesses find they must continually innovate in order to survive. They are training all their organizational members in innovative, and they reward innovative behavior. When organizations attune themselves to environmental changes they begin systematically learning at a deeper level. This sets the groundwork for continuous transformation. (Porras and Silvers 1991, 54). They fine tune their organizations to continuously identify changes and learn how to respond early. This is the skill we see in the tribe of Issachar. All were trained to discern the times and know how to react in an innovative new way. This powerful "modern" concept of continuous transformation was already in use, thousands of years ago.

Innovative transformation starts by understanding the gaps (strategic drift) between the organization and the changes in the environment (Accenture 2012). We recognize our environment is in a state of constant change (Cornish 2004). Transformation is an ongoing, continual process of adjusting to the journey (Accenture 2012). When we drive for continuous transformation, we create a multiplier effect in which changes cascade out in multiple directions (Senge 2006; Colegrove 2011). This doesn't just change the organization, but it also begins to change the entire environment (Senge 2006; Colegrove 2011). Training an army of innovative leaders like the leaders of Issachar creates good soil in which these multiplier effects may sprout. The goal is not to find one innovative leader, but to create an entire organization of transformative leaders. God give us the faith to make this happen.

CHAPTER 5

A FEW FUNDAMENTALS

"You proved that you could be trusted with a small amount. I will put you in charge of a large amount." Matthew 25:23 (GW)

RESEARCH AND GOD'S WILL

Seeking God starts with prayer, but it doesn't end there. God called many Biblical characters to perform research as a complimentary part of discerning God's plan. Moses was told to send spies out into the land of Canaan (Num 13). God revealed battle plans to Joshua only after he had performed research (Josh 5). At another time, Joshua failed to do his research and made an improper alliance with imposters, posing as people from a distant land (Josh 9:5). God revealed the methodology for rebuilding the walls only after Nehemiah performed research regarding the state of the walls. Research, then, is a Biblical part of hearing and discerning the Lord's leading.

Research should fuel our faith for what God will do. Problems arose when Moses' twelve spies came back with the results of their research and lost faith in God's intervention. God was so angry with their response that he forced them to return to wandering the desert.

God has empowered his people to research all that is done under heaven, and the accumulated wisdom from this research is called a gift from God (Ecc 13:1). This wisdom teaches us right from wrong (Psalm 37:30), is a gift to those with discernment (Prov 14:6), and comes from giving careful thought to our ways (Prov 14:8). Proverbs 4:7 states, "wisdom is supreme, therefore get wisdom" (NIV). Secular writers state that wisdom is the "most crucial talent" (Pfeffer & Sutton 2006, Kindle location 2073) which comes from both "knowing what you know and knowing what you don't know" (Pfeffer & Sutton 2006, Kindle location 2065). Research is simply the process of learning what we know and what we don't.

Research is supposed to be the basis for every single decision made within the health-care industry through a process called evidence-based decision making. (Pfeffer & Sutton 2006). Before this, doctors were performing surgeries, nurses were taking action, and hospitals were enacting policies because common sense dictated it must be done in a certain way. It turns out that this common sense, which everyone knew, frequently turned out to be dangerously wrong—and many times, deadly. The movement to base every decision upon solid research was started to make hospitals safer, improve quality of care and reduce deaths.

The more evidence based decision making is used, the more we find that much of popular thought is actually contradictory to reality. Instead of making decisions because "everyone does it this way," or because "we've always done it this way," all decisions should be backed by research. This process has revolutionized hospitals, dramatically improving their effectiveness.

The remarkable improvements in the health industry caused the business world to take notice (Pfeffer and Sutton 2006). As business leaders began integrating research into every aspect of their decision-making process, they found that much of their popular management techniques were also flat-out wrong, and many times, even destructive. A movement formed to create a culture of informed decisions. Businesses began finding a significant gap between what they knew and what they did.

Here's an example of how even billion dollar corporations can get caught into the trap of doing something simply because "everyone knows" it's a good thing. Decades of research shows that more than 70 percent of mergers fail to bring the expected economic benefits (Pfeffer and Sutton 2006). More often than not, the merger inflicts significant damage to both organizations. This readily available information has not slowed the breakneck speed of mega-mergers and buy-outs we see in the business world.

Possibly the most famous failed merger in history is the AOL-Time Warner merger in 2000 (Arango 2010). Announced as a historic merger in the age of new media, it soon ended creating the largest recorded financial losses in business history. Thousands of people were laid off; countless retirement accounts were destroyed. Despite this research, executives still chose to believe the popular wisdom which states that mergers are a sure path to economic dominance.

Paul supports this concept as he warns Timothy against simply seeking evidence which supports his own point of view (2 Tim 4:3). Proverbs urge us to pursue data and information as a necessary part of our pursuit of wisdom (Prov 15:22; 11:14). Proverbs also tell us that it is a noble pursuit to search out the heart of a matter (Prov 25:2). Proverbs calls those who ignore research, "fools" who take no pleasure in understanding (Prov 18:2; 1:7).

As Paul warned Timothy, we cannot merely seek data which supports our assumptions. Our mind, however, has a terrible propensity to filter out data which conflicts with our existing point of view (Pfeffer and Sutton 2006). Evidence based decision making includes actively seeking out information which could challenge our ideas. This is the cornerstone of the scientific method: seek to disprove that which you desire to prove. Information should fuel every aspect of our decision making. We don't have time for the mistakes we'll make if we leave the research out. Research is a critical part of seeking God's will.

CREATIVE DESTRUCTION

This next concept is vitally important.

Capitalist economies work because of a process described as "creative destruction" (Schumpeter 1942, 139). To stay ahead and keep from falling into the gap of strategic drift, organizations and industries must constantly recreate themselves. This creative process results in a constant flow of new, better, and more efficient products and services. Companies refusing to innovate get left behind, or destroyed by other's creativity. The creativity of one company or organization causes the destruction of another.

Some might find the concept ruthless, yet without it, we'd still be writing on animal skins, riding on horses, and making pictures on the walls of caves. Instead, we write on sophisticated electronic devices, ride in comfortable automobiles with internal combustion engines, and create pictures on our hand-held devices. The process of creative destruction creates a ceaseless forward march of new products and new opportunities. As the world gets more integrated, the innovation process gets faster and faster.

Walmart's creative ability to re-design the way it distributes and warehouses products all but destroyed other retailers who couldn't compete with Walmart's efficiency, like K-mart. Amazon (for better or worse) is creatively destroying local bookstores as well as the traditional publishing industry. Now, through same-day shipping, Amazon might just do to Walmart what Walmart did to K-mart (Manjoo 2013).

At the fundamental level, sales measure the desirability of a company's products (Collins 2005). If people no longer want the product, the organization

47

is forced to innovate and create something more desirable. Otherwise, it faces being creatively destroyed.

Kodak is an unfortunate example. In just a few short years the multi-billion dollar film company was driven to bankruptcy by the "fad" of digital photography (Shayon 2013). Fuji, however, saw digital photography as the wave of the future, and just like the tribe of Issachar, positioned itself favorably within that new market. Interestingly, the success of Fuji's digital products hastened the end of its film business. In essence, Fuji film creatively destructed itself and formed into a new digital company in order to survive. Yet Fuji saw the digital future, and decided it was better to emerge as a leader in a new market, than protect their large share of a dying market.

While creative destruction drives innovation in for-profit businesses, most ministries and non-profits are fundamentally different in their design; money and sales are not a measure of the desirability of their services (Collins 2005). In most cases, the people receiving the "services" are not the ones paying the full cost for those services. Instead, donors pay, while someone else receives the benefit. Donors rarely even meet the recipients. As a result, ministries are largely immune from the process of creative destruction.

For example: an outreach teaches underprivileged children to read in a poor country. The ministry is small, and growing. It's difficult to judge the quality of the literacy projects this ministry provides. If people paid, one could judge the quality or value of the program by seeing how much people were willing to pay, but donors cover these costs because of the economic conditions of the recipients. The program reports back to donors the number of people attending their literacy program. Yet there may be a variety of reasons people attend, maybe there are fun activities; perhaps people simply attend when there is nothing else for them to do, and attendance is so sporadic that no real learning ever happens. The economics of a ministry are fundamentally different than a for-profit company. Unlike for-profit organizations, the value of ministry activity is incredibly difficult to measure. How do we measure the degree of social transformation? How do we put a dollar value on conversions or churches planted? All are poor indicators of the quality of work performed by the missionary or organization.

Likewise, competition does not impact ministry the same way as it does other for-profit companies. Because even the best feedback given to donors is limited, donors won't necessarily divert funds to other organizations because another ministry is doing a better job. Something else drives donations. Ministry donations are primarily driven by the non-profit's ability to tell transformational stories (Collins

2005). To give you an example of how this works, imagine a for-profit company making mosquito nets for African countries. This company must manufacture a high quality/low cost product, pay for transporting and importing, marketing, etc. The mosquito nets must be sold at a price local people can afford. If the company cannot make money, the company will go out of business. Efficiency drives the organization to sell enough nets at a reasonable price so that they can pay salaries and hopefully make a profit in the process. .

To this company, cost per mosquito net sold is an extremely important number. The company will lose money if a competitor can sell comparable nets at a cheaper price. If that happens, the company can either reduce its own prices (entering a destructive price war with its competitor), or it can hope people will pay more for higher quality nets, or it can try selling specialty nets for niche uses (Daft 2003). It is important to understand, that competition leads to better products and/or better prices. Companies unable to do this are creatively destroyed out of the marketplace (monopolies are a different story. Without competition, the result is generally higher prices and/or lower quality products).

Now consider a non-profit ministry providing mosquito nets for Africa. Because malaria in Africa is such a hot topic, this non-profit sends its donors the story of how a single mosquito net saved a child's life from malaria (what could be more moving and transformational than saving an innocent child's life?). One story like this can drive donations for years. Donors, however, have little (if any) knowledge regarding the quality of the net, the cost per net, or how long they hold up under the conditions in which they are used.

Theoretically speaking, the ministry could have tremendous waste in every area of production, transportation and distribution, and the donors would never know. There's no direct competition for the nets (they're given away for free), so there's no direct pressure to keep costs as low as possible. Sales don't provide feedback to the organization on how desirable these nets are versus other nets. As a result, there's no pressure to innovate and make better nets. Because the net is free to the recipient, the recipient doesn't care if the non-profit's internal price per net is $5 or $50. Without the process of creative destruction, inefficient ministries can continue for years, long after a for-profit model would have been creatively destroyed by a new, more efficient organization.

That's not to say the non-profit model is a bad model, but it's important to understand the implications of the dynamics. In the absence of market pressures, donor dollars can continue to fund projects long after they've lost their usefulness, effectiveness, or efficiency. It may cost the non-profit ten times more to produce and ship a net to Africa than it does for local African companies to make and sell a better quality net. But it doesn't matter. The ministry is insulated from the natural process of creative destruction and as a result, there is no driving force pressing the ministry to constantly innovate in order to survive. It is good that ministries don't face the same pressures, but the downside is that ministries don't have the same cues that their projects have lasted far past their expiration dates.

This isn't to say that non-profit ministries are totally devoid of the pressure to innovate. Just as with for-profit companies, pressures to innovate go back to financial pressures. It is the donation collecting side of the ministry which feels the greatest pressure to innovate, as this is the side affected by market forces. If donations cease, the organization ceases to exist. Therefore we generally see much more innovation on this side of the ministry. Organizations are continuously looking for new and better ways to tell and distribute stories (direct mail has moved to email, video, social media, and online presence) and new and easier methods of collecting donations (checks have changed to online donations, PayPal, crowd funding, and probably coming soon, Bitcoin).

For-profit businesses must retune themselves to every slight change in their environment in order to avoid creative destruction (Schumpeter 1942). But non-profits can continue to provide services as long as their stories of transformation continue to attract donations. The environment in which the ministry provides its services could change suddenly and drastically; yet if the old stories of transformation keep donations steady, the organization could continue to operate long after its mosquito nets (or other services) have become irrelevant. Strategic drift won't be as much of a factor on the distribution side as it is on the side attracting donations. If donations begin to decrease, the pain will be felt much more quickly—hence the innovation on the side attracting donations.

It's not that donors to mission organizations don't derive any benefit from their donations. They do, but they are intangible in nature (Collins 2005). The donor receives a good feeling for saving a child from malaria, obeying God in helping accomplish the great commission, or knowing that they are investing in treasures in heaven. Through stories of transformation, donors know they've helped transform a life, plant a church, or simply been obedient to God. These stories are, by and large, the only feedback donors receive as to whether there has been an equitable transaction in return for the donation (Allee 2003). To state it simply, stories let donors decide whether their donations are worth it or not (Collins 2005). These stories do not necessarily depend on the missionary being a good missionary, instead, they depend on the missionary being a good story teller. Hence, many missionaries can survive without innovating as long as they can continue to tell what is perceived as a valuable story.

None of this should minimize the fact that God is the source of our funding. "Once I was young, and now I am old. Yet I have never seen the godly abandoned or their children begging for bread" (NLT). I have seen God provide for missionaries who tell stories well, as well as those who do not. I have also seen God provide in innovative ways for individuals who are chronically underfunded. Certainly God moves upon people's hearts to donate and provide. Yet we do see a difference in support levels with individuals and organizations that consistently communicate what God is doing through their organizations in an effective manner.

Churches are a special breed of non-profit (Kroll 2003). Unlike the mosquito net example, church donors receive (at least in-part) a direct benefit from their contributions. The weekly worship experience provides a spiritual benefit for church donors. If church members don't like the worship experience, or the preaching, etc., they'll likely leave and take their donations with them. In this sense, Church donors function as consumers of the ministry which the church provides. Examining the flow of money and services received, it resembles a for-profit business model (Allee 2003). This means there are some degrees of competitive forces at work when it comes to church attendance and are more vulnerable to creative destruction than other non-profit ministries (Schumpeter 1942). While churches themselves don't try to compete with each other, attendees do have a propensity to move to another church if their current one is not meeting their own spiritual needs. As such, there is more pressure on churches to innovate, than other ministries where donations are disconnected from recipients.

This isn't actually such a bad thing. Remember the European theologian McGrath? God wants the church to minister to people. I'm not a fan of church hopping or of church splits, but if a church legitimately cannot meet the changing spiritual needs of its people, most members will eventually go somewhere else. If a church loses people, hopefully the church will begin innovating the way it meets people's spiritual needs. As we mentioned before, when churches get locked into old ways of ministering to people, ways that are no longer effective, they languish. If they languish long enough, they'll eventually die. Strategic drift leads to creative destruction.

This type of creative destruction has brought a host of benefits to the modern church. These include contemporary worship experiences, online Bible study tools, recovery groups, house groups, relevant discipleship methods, and countless other resources. These were all developed as churches sought to fill the spiritual gaps existing in the culture.

So what's the point?

The point isn't to simply learn how to tell good stories—although there are many who need to do so. The point is that our world is rapidly changing and even the best businesses are falling behind increasing chasms of strategic drift. Without a natural mechanism forcing our ministries to continuously innovate, we are especially vulnerable to perpetuating outdated programs aimed at yesterday's needs, as long as we keep telling compelling stories. Because non-profits lack this feedback loop, we need to be all the more vigilant to pay attention to the changes happening around us. Our objective should be to fulfill God's calling in a way that understands the times. We should be fervently praying that God teaches us use the creativity he placed within us to creatively meet the needs of His children, in the ways he wants those needs to be met.

Ministry effectiveness is a tricky thing to measure. Is the missionary laboring for fifteen years without any converts any less effective than the one seeing hundreds turn to Christ? Effectiveness is simply staying true to what the voice of God is telling us to do. There are many times, however, when we realize we can do what we are doing better. I'm reminded of Jethro coming to Moses' side and saying, "You'll never care for everyone's needs this way. Let me show you a better way" (Exodus 18:17–23).

CHALLENGING OUR ASSUMPTIONS

In order to become innovators, we need to push our learning and problem-solving skills down to a deeper level. Most often, our learning simply happens on the surface level, bound by the inadequately informed assumptions we carry. As a result, most change is merely incremental in nature (Cummings and Worley 2009). For example, the cost to ship mosquito nets to Africa is rising. One solution is learning about negotiation skills to reduce the prices paid for shipping or raw materials, or one could combine multiple shipments together with other shipments. The result is an incremental improvement. Surface learning merely copes with visible problems (Boa 2011). It rarely deals with the underlying issues, structures or systems. Deeper learning digs down, identifying and challenging the underlying assumptions we carry (Argyris 1997).

Psychologist Larry Crabb states, "Most of us make it through life by coping, not changing" (Crabb 1992, 31). A gambler copes by asking friends to help him stay away from casinos, but this does not solve his problem. Another option would be to dig deeper, exploring the underlying reasons why he gambles. A twelve-step program challenges his assumptions about God, life, and the world around him. The goal, of course, is total transformation. Transformation only happens with deeper learning and challenging assumptions.

The modern washing machine is a great example. Most changes in product design coped with surface issues. As manufacturers sought more energy-efficient machines, they added computer controlled timers (Wikipedia 2014). Then they changed the way they churned and spun the clothes. All these were incremental changes—variations within a theme. They didn't challenge the basic assumptions about how clothes are actually washed.

Then came LG Corporation, who wanted to dramatically cut the amount of time and energy it took to remove stains and wash clothes. LG questioned everything. They found the entire industry was locked into one single assumption: washing machines must use water. Initially, this assumption seems absurd—"of course you must use water." Yet LG tried a host of new and innovative ideas, and settled on steam, which increased washing performance by 21 percent while reducing both electricity and the amount of water used in the process. Digging deeper and identifying and challenging our assumptions allows us to find breakthrough solutions (Argyris 1997). It requires taking a step back to explore why things work the way they do. It requires questioning the deep seated assumptions we hold about how to address the issues. In this way, LG threw off the shackles of traditional thinking and began experimenting with radical, new, innovative, and industry changing ideas.

The Pharisees came to Christ with their surface level problems. On one occasion, they asked him whether they should pay taxes to Caesar (Matt 22). Jesus, however, refused to be trapped by their constraining surface assumptions. Instead, Jesus dug deeper and challenged their underlying values. "Whose image is this?" he replied, "And whose inscription? . . . give back to Caesar what is Caesar's" (Matt 22:20–21).

Here's a real-world ministry example. A denomination was experiencing a church planting movement where thousands of churches were being planted in a remote area of the world. If a pastor showed skill in planting numerous churches, they would provide this pastor with a seminary education. But, as thousands of new pastors emerged, each starting many, many churches, they couldn't keep up with the need for education. In the past, they had sent seminary professors to this country to provide occasional theological training, but there was an increasing strain on the limited number of seminary professors who both spoke the language and had the time to travel—and the hostile political climate made it difficult for their professors to reliably obtain visas. Shipping seminary books became prohibitively expensive. Books sent there were often destroyed in tropical storms. The Internet wasn't an option, as it simply wasn't available.

A denominational leader said, "We were scratching our heads. There was not enough consistency in our training and our professors were not consistent in traveling to these countries." They were stuck in a mode of coping with surface issues, hoping for incremental changes such as: "How can we send more professors?" "How can we ship more books?" "How can we protect the books from tropical storms?" Then they began questioning their assumptions. Some of their questions appeared silly at first. "Are books necessary for seminary education?" They started to find inspiration. They imagined an e-book, pre-loaded with everything the students needed. This solved most of their problems: Internet access, shipping, housing a library, etc. Then they asked, "Do we need to send professors?" To answer this issue, they asked graduates to become mentors of small groups of other pastors. Any tests could simply be written and mailed.

Now, several years later, there are over two thousand e-books in use around this country. Despite never even seeing a computer, emerging pastors are able to become familiar with their new electronic devices in just two days. Regional leaders report students learn faster than ever before. What's more, these devices dramatically cut their time for sermon preparation, allowing them more time to spend with their families and parishioners. As is so often the case, transformative solutions are both simple and elegant (Oster 2011). When we begin challenging assumptions, we must make the "previously undiscussable [sic] problems discussable," while "interrupting the closed cycle of defensive reasoning and behavior" (Argyris 1997, 304). Transformational thinking can be scary because it exposes us to the loving scrutiny of others and bumps into other people's assumptions. Defensive behavior will shut down innovative ideas and builds walls around deep seated assumptions, while maintaining the status quo.

Every plan or idea is based upon a set of assumptions (Dewar 2002). An assumption could be as simple as "we will have the people and resources to finish our plan." Another is that "this people group will still be speaking this language when we finish this Bible translation." Another is "if we don't do something about this issue, no one else will." These assumptions may or may not be true. Most of the time, we don't consciously recognize that we even hold these assumptions. We subconsciously assume them to be true. Identifying and challenging them, however, is an important part of the innovation process. Many innovations only come when we specifically identify that which constraining our thinking.

Digging wells is a familiar scenario for Christian ministries overseas, but a North American non-profit found an innovative way to challenge assumptions about the process and unearthed a brilliant solution (Mattson 2013). Everyone was facing the same issue. Existing well digging machines were prohibitively expensive and too large to get into all the remote locations needing access to water. There was no way to drill all the wells necessary with existing technologies. Other organizations sought incremental improvements in the weight of the well digging machinery, but this organization, began identifying and questioning assumptions. The first assumption they identified was that large powerful machinery was necessary to drill the wells. Many said it could not be done, but still, they enlisted the help of a local university's mechanical engineering department, challenging them to create a portable, human powered well digging machine. It took a while, but the university eventually devised a human powered well digger, easily disassembled and transportable by small plane, pickup truck, or even a horse drawn cart.

The second assumption was that non-profits such as their own were the only ones who cared about the problem. Questioning this thought, the team searched for African businesses who might also be interested in the problem, and could help manufacturing the devices at a reduced rate. They were surprised to find many willing to help. Today these well diggers are made in Africa and sent to remote villages with minimal cost. Because they were willing to entertain the "silly" questions and challenge deep seated assumptions, many remote villages are gaining access to water.

The human powered Village Drill. Mattson 2013.

As another example, a medical missionary desired to perform cataract surgeries for people living in a remote village in Nepal. He began identifying his assumptions. One of which was whether his team members would be willing or able to eat the Nepali food for a full two weeks. To protect against this assumption, he plans the trip around good restaurants he knows. Secretly, he also packs each team member's favorite comfort snack foods just in case they get sick.

Another assumption is that the team will be able to get the visas they need amid the tumultuous political situation. The team jokingly asks if they really had to fly fifteen hours. Of course the team needs to fly, but they began checking this assumption.

They find that a nearby Indian city provides cataract surgeries at low cost. It would cost the team of doctors $30,000 to fly to Nepal and perform the surgeries; but it would only cost them $8,000 to pay for the Nepali to cross the border and have the surgery in an Indian hospital. Further investigation showed that the team could donate $40,000 for equipment and a local Nepalese hospital could then perform the surgeries themselves. They could solve this immediate issue by spending much less money, or they could spend a little more and provide long-term transformation.

Our own pre-conceptions limit us from recognizing the sub-conscious assumptions we hold. We simply say, "That could never happen." I remember talking to a vice president of a well-respected ministry. I asked, "What if something happened to the president, would you be prepared?" He responded, "That won't happen." Shortly thereafter, the president became ill and was no longer able to continue in his position. It was then, that the executive team realized a terrible secret, the organization was carrying a staggering amount of internal debt to designated funds. The president assumed he could resolve the problem without worrying the rest of the executive team. Yet as the problem grew, his health deteriorated. In a few short weeks, the organization not only lost its president, but also went from a place of perceived health to an alarming crisis. It took years for them to recover.

There are a tremendous amount assumptions which were made in this real-life scenario. The rest of the executive team assumed the organization was healthy and didn't go beyond the organization's bottom line health. They also assumed there was adequate transparency; that no one on a ministry's executive team would hide anything of importance. What other assumptions might you identify from this real-life scenario?

There's an exercise some organizations are learning to go through called "kill our company" or "kill the strategy." Basically, several hours to a half a day are set aside to examine various trends and imagine how they might interact to seriously disrupt the organization or its strategies. Part of this time is used to explore unexpected events which could also seriously damage the organization. Some brainstormed questions might include, "What if one of our members was taken hostage?" "What if a member of our senior leadership was caught abusing children?" "What if our leadership team all died in a crash on the way to a conference?" "What if a member of the senior leadership is hiding an important issue?" One organization had just asked themselves a few of these questions, when someone brought up a recent article they had seen about child abuse happening in another ministry. Through the ensuing lawsuits, the once vibrant, cutting edge ministry was now struggling for its very survival. Suddenly, this threat seemed very plausible.

The process of challenging our assumptions lets us realize we have much more influence over our situations than previously realized (Bishop 2000). The process helps organizations identify areas with greater influence and a host of opportunities for bringing transformation (Dewar 2002). It also helps organizations be prepared to deal with a wide variety of scenarios.

Identifying and challenging assumptions can start out as a relatively simple exercise (Bishop 2000). Begin asking questions from a variety of viewpoints and perspectives. Look for the boundaries which tend to constrain your thinking. As you begin identifying assumptions, write these assumptions down. Then research and get others involved in finding a solution. Set aside some time to explore scenarios which could kill the organization. Who knows, maybe you'll find local businesses or colleges care about the same issue as well.

SYSTEMS THINKING

We exist in a complex environment comprised of various cultures, governments, organizations, corporations, donors, recipients, etc. To find truly innovative solutions, we must learn to understand our environment as a complex, interconnected whole (Senge 2006). Nothing happens in a vacuum. Every action creates ripple effects in multiple directions. All too often we oversimplify our environment.

One organization had a goal of alleviating malnutrition through large scale agricultural assistance (sending grain and other staples) (Corbett & Fikkert 2009). In the beginning, they saw a substantial decrease in deaths, particularly among infants and the elderly. With this early success, the program gained tremendous support. With such a rapid and dramatic decrease in mortality, the population grew substantially. Within a few short years malnutrition was an even bigger problem than before. The difference was that now, the region was already deeply dependent on agricultural assistance. Ending the program would be catastrophic for the local peoples. This real-world problem shows how malnutrition is part of a system. Simply attempting to solve the problem through the most obvious solution (giving food) created ripple effects which made the problem worse. Altering one part of the system without understanding the interconnected whole usually produces unintended consequences (Corbett and Fikkert 2009). Before going in and changing something, every effort should be directed at understanding the system underlying the present problem.

Here is another true ministry story highlighting the need to understand the underlying systems at work before getting involved. There were four churches in a remote valley of a distant country. All the working aged adults had moved off to factories for work, and all the youth lived in boarding schools in the cities. Only the very old and very young were left behind in the villages. These four churches had been planted fifteen years earlier. Attendance steadily fell as people left to the cities for school, work, or as they died. No one ever expected anything from these churches.

These churches began seeking God through prayer and fasting. At the end of thirty days, they were convinced that God wanted them to plant a church in every one of the three hundred villages of their county. They mobilized everyone in their church to go into to the surrounding villages and to share the good news of Christ. Before long there were a few new converts, and one pastor sent half his congregation to plant a church in the neighboring village. The grandmothers cried, believing the pastor was maliciously breaking up their church. The following Sunday, however, the new church AND the original church each had as many people as there were in the original church meeting—God effectively doubled their numbers in a single week! These same grandmothers cried with tears of joy that God was actively building his church. Excited with their early success, these (now five) churches met together and made a plan to multiply churches throughout their county. In their first year, they planted more than twenty churches. In the next six months they planted more than twenty-five house churches. They were well on their way to reaching all three hundred villages. It seemed nothing could stop this burgeoning movement.

Then, a devastating earthquake struck the neighboring province. Tens of thousands died. Even though their own county hadn't seen any destruction,

Christians came from other provinces into the region to rebuild houses. After learning that there weren't any houses to build there, they inquired of the spiritual condition of the region. They were astounded to find such a high number of brand new house churches. "These Christians are so poor," they thought, "They cannot even afford a proper church. Here they all are, simply meeting in homes and the pastors aren't even supported by the ministry." They asked these local believers if they wanted money to rent a larger space in which to conduct proper church services and assistance for the pastors to quit their jobs and become full time. "Yes!" they responded eagerly.

Within a very short time, money was sent to rent office space in more than forty locations around the county. Everyone in the villages participated in converting the rented space into a proper church. The outsiders couldn't be more pleased with what they started. They told their stories of how they were helping support these rural pastors. What they didn't know, however, was that they had successfully diverted attention away from evangelizing the other three hundred villages. At that moment, all church planting activity stopped as members focused on renovating their newly acquired space. The local pastors who had started the initial movement re-grouped, trying to re-mobilize their lay army. In the years that followed, only a handful of new house churches were planted. A movement died in the hands of the well intentioned outsiders. This story does have a happy, albeit awkward, ending. The outsiders eventually became frustrated and upset that these local pastors were not planting new churches as before. In their anger, they eventually pulled all their funding for the office space and salaries. Churches were forced to return to meeting in homes. Pastors went back to being bi-vocational. Within a very short time, they began planting new house churches again.

This is an example of the law of unintended consequences. Changing the dynamics of a system without understanding the system itself, produces unintended ripple effects. Change was brought in from the outside without knowing the dynamics of the local system.

It is easy to address the surface needs seen from the outside while thinking we're making an impact. What we create, however, is often much different than what we intend (Senge 2006). It's easy to count the number of people fed or the number of church buildings erected. It's much more difficult to understand the true consequences of our "help." "Cause and effect are not closely related in time and space," writes Senge in *The Fifth Discipline* (2006, 62). As outsiders, we must be extremely careful lest our help hinder or even dismantle a greater move of

God. It is all too easy for North Americans to believe their financial resources can solve any problem.

Meanwhile, true, high impact leverage points are rarely obvious (Senge 2006). The amount of energy required to turn the front of the ship is enormous. Yet a tiny rudder can do the job, that is, if you understand you must turn it in the opposite direction of your intended destination. Leverage points aren't obvious, and sometimes you need to move in a direction contrary to your intended destination. Our best intentions can stop the movement of God and we won't even know it. Time, prayer, and research are our best friends.

In order to find the proper place to engage, we must stop thinking in terms of linear causes and effects and begin thinking about interrelationships between all the complex parts (Senge 2006). Outside resources, whether it be grain or money, create ripple effects through the systems. It doesn't mean we don't give; it may mean we give seeds and irrigation equipment instead. Even then, we must be careful lest we take jobs away from others selling seeds locally.

Some systems create balance (such as a gyroscope), while other systems cascade and reinforce change (such as in chain reactions). If you bump into a balancing system, the system will push back. For instance, if you try and distract me while I'm concentrating on my writing, I'll instinctively push back as my brain tries to maintain concentration. If you give more responsibility to a team already trying to balance their existing responsibilities, the team will push back against the added disruption.

In the story about malnutrition, there was an unhealthy balance between food and deaths. Adding more food to the system merely changed the boundaries of the unhealthy balance. The new system was set for greater malnutrition later, while also being dependent on outside resources.

The story about the churches multiplying was an example of cascading change. The more churches they planted, the more people became involved in the process, resulting in even more churches planted. Bringing in outside resources changed the dynamics of the system. The system shifted from cascading growth to balancing while maintaining buildings and programs. Removing the outside finances removed the boundaries creating the balancing system, and churches began multiplying again.

If we encounter resistance to change, the key is not to push harder. Instead, we should seek leverage elsewhere (Senge 2006). When old, tried and true methods stop working, our tendency is to simply try harder but we fail to realize the dynamics of the system have fundamentally changed. Pressing harder often only creates frustration and increased resistance. As an outside observer, it is all too easy to assume we know how to fix a problem (Senge 2006). Simple solutions, without knowledge regarding the complex interrelated systems which create the problem, lead to the law of unintended consequences.

Here is another example. Our team had been working overseas for ten years to help multiply churches (Seipp 2013). Local pastors wanted our help to plant new churches, but they were locked into a top-down style of leadership that refused to relinquish control. New leaders were micromanaged in a way that stifled initiative. They lacked a feeling of any responsibility. We used a variety of teaching methods, tried aiming at different learning styles, and anything else we could think of. We kept looking for new leverage points. We talked, we questioned, we researched, etc. The pastors knew they needed to change, but just couldn't figure out how. We fasted, we prayed, we sought the Lord. Then, the answer came through an unexpected conversation. I discussed these challenges with an old friend, a local university professor. I had hoped the conversation would help me understand the social systems that were reinforcing their specific leadership behaviors. My question developed into a three day conversation. The professor explained how specific cultural ideals shaped the thinking patterns of all leaders throughout their society, not just the pastors with whom I was working. Their leadership reflected their overarching social structures, creating a balancing system. Any efforts to change that system would face resistance (just as we had faced). More importantly, even if we did succeed in changing a few leaders, cultural norms would either eventually push them back into the old system, or the changes would likely not cascade into the next generation of leaders. Instead of working against such a resistant reinforcing system, we were encouraged to find a way to work within the system. We were encouraged to find local business leaders who had fostered responsibility and initiative in their own employees. Then we would apply what we learned in and through the church. This professor was urging us not to push harder against a resistant balancing system, but to seek out other leverage points already existing within the culture that would help us achieve our goals.

S CURVES

Practically everything from animals, to trees, to governments, countries, businesses, and even product ideas follow a natural growth cycle. Because of its shape, the cycle is called the S curve (Modis 1994). Earlier in this book, an S curve was used to show the growth and development of various countries' missionary sending.

This natural, gently flowing curve describes stages of development, growth, maturity and eventual decline. The S curve has been called a universal descriptor of life cycles. The beginning part of the S curve represents a season of infancy and total dependency on others. Children turn the corner as they are able to take care of themselves and begin applying what they learn. Young adulthood up until middle age represents the steepest part of the curve, the season of greatest learning, vitality and productivity. In advanced years, people gradually slow down. Eventually, they turn a corner to become increasingly dependent upon others. Ecclesiastes 3 states that for everything, there is a season. There are seasons for planting and harvesting, just as there are seasons for being born and dying.

S Curve

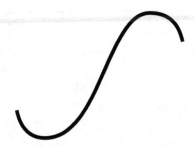

S curves are often used to describe life cycles of products. The Sony Walkman was one of the first portable tape players. When it was first introduced, it was very expensive and few people purchased it. It took time, but costs went down and its popularity soared. At one point, it seemed as if everyone was buying one; this represents the steepest part of the S curve. Soon, Panasonic other companies introduced competing products, and competition brought down the cost even lower. Eventually the market became saturated as small Taiwanese companies produced inexpensive personal tape players. Everyone was making one and, it seemed, everyone had one. Sales and profits decreased.

Death, however, need not be a foregone conclusion. Innovation reignites a new S curve on top of an old one. Sometimes this is done by adding new features which entice people to buy a newer version. New features were added to the portable tape player throughout the 80's. Headphones were improved, igniting a new S curve. Then Dolby sound was added, igniting yet another S curve. AM/FM radios were added, then shortwave. Each addition was strategically introduced to reignite new sales and get consumers to upgrade to a better model. The same happens with everything from cell phones, cars, appliances, clothes, etc. Upgrading can happen over and over again, but because these are incremental improvements, they only go so far as strategic drift increases. Eventually an entirely new product will come in to take its place.

Most assume that the best time to begin investing in innovation is when old products lose their steam and crest the top of the S curve. This is a huge mistake. No one knows which new innovative ideas will become successful, and it takes time for new ideas to develop and mature. The best time to begin innovating is when existing products enter the fast growth period, which is the steepest section of the S curve and the greatest amount of success is being realized (Handy 1994). While some may think this creates distraction, it actually ensures continued, uninterrupted growth. When we begin innovating early, we allow time for our new ideas to develop through the early side of the S curve.

Our goal is to overlap the S curves so that we minimize downtime. By the time the old ideas are cresting the S curve, a new innovative idea should be entering its fast growth stage. This ensures uninterrupted growth from one program to the next.

Overlapping S Curves

During the fast growth stage, excess funds available. If these funds are merely funneled back into the fast growing product, they will realize a smaller and smaller return on their investment. As the product crests the S curve, they are pumping so much money into the product with nothing to show in return. Instead, they should have used a portion of their funds for the development of new ideas. Waiting too late to innovate is a fatal mistake that all too many organizations make. It is difficult to innovate when organizations are cutting costs or laying off people. Many companies who wait too long never recover.

S Curve in Delayed Innovation

Wondering what this could have to do with ministry? Everything. Go back and review the eras of mission history. Notice how each era took time to form? Notice that the eras overlap? As one era was slowing down, another era was ramping up. William Carey was certainly not the first missionary, he followed the example of the Moravians. Yet, he was the right person at the right time for ushering in the rapid growth of the S curve of the first era of missions. God, in his wisdom has orchestrated a cascading set of mission S curves, so that His kingdom continues to expand.

In 2016, many mission organizations and missionaries are finding it more and more difficult to raise funds. Old funding models seem to have crested the S curve. Unfortunately, it's fairly late in the game to begin developing new, innovative strategies. Crowd-funding took the secular world by storm a few years ago, yet few Christian organizations have even attempted a crowd-funding strategy. The time to begin experimenting should have started several years ago, yet many mission organizations failed to see any need to change when times were good. Innovating early would have allowed new funding models to mature and grow by the time previous models tapered off. As a result, many organizations are now finding themselves in a difficult situation. They need to innovate, but there are fewer resources available to do so.

Life stages and cycles are a great example of overlapping S curves. Most mammals are not fertile during their initial stages of fundamental rapid development. Imagine if six-year-olds had babies, or if three-month old puppies had their own puppies. At this age, the youngsters are still unable to care for themselves. It's also a blessing that fertility ends in old age because at a certain point, it takes all one's energy to care for oneself. Reproduction happens during the most productive, steepest part of the S curve, so that there is adequate energy to care for the next generation.

The fashion industry is another example, and one that has built in creative destruction to speed up the process. The fashion industry already has the next popular styles planned out well in advance. If you want to see what we will find popular to wear next year, go to Asia, where the clothing factories are. Here, people make the clothes which will fill next year's shelves. Those clothes took time to design and the designers are already preparing several years in advance. Shorts are long and baggy in solid colors, then next year they are short and tight in plaid. The following year they are long and baggy in plaid, and then they are short with solid colors. The industry goes back and forth, knowing that people won't want to wear something that is so obviously out of date. They creatively destroy the old styles, so that people will throw their old clothes away from last year and buy something new this year. If the industry rode out the fashion S curve until it died, before introducing a new fashion, it would take a year or more to design, and manufacture, and market the new style.

Cascading S Curve

As stated in a previous chapter, mission sending in the United States has likely crested its current S curve. We've passed the time when we saw rapid increases in the sending of new missionaries. All indicators point to a coming decline. The best time to have begun exploring new models for recruiting and sending missionaries would have been when growth rates were high. During that time, multiple models for sending could be developed and explored. Praise God, the rise of majority world missions is counteracting the decline in sending from the States.

If agencies wait till there's a significant drop in mission sending, funds may be too tight to spend on new recruiting initiatives. Under these circumstances, trying new ideas carries greater risk. For this reason and more, it's very likely that we could see a surge of mergers (or even closures) within the mission industry as agencies deal with an emerging new reality. Shortly after I originally wrote about this possibility, Latin America Mission merged with United World Mission.

Initiatives on the field don't last forever. Ideas will only work for so long. After a while, expend more and more effort for fewer and fewer results. When this happens, we know we've crested the S curve and strategic drift is beginning to grow.

Sometimes, all we need is an innovative spark to start a new S curve and revitalize our ministry. Other times, entirely new strategies are needed. There are only so many times that new life can be breathed into old strategies. Eventually we need new wineskins to hold new wine (Luke 5:37–38).

William Carey's coastland strategy was innovative, and the strategy lasted for a long while. Later, Hudson Taylor moved inland and sparked a new S curve with inland missions. Likewise, Lausanne sparked the fire of mobilizing native mission movements. Now that those movements have been mobilized, we're poised to start a new S curve.

Social justice seems to be part of a new S curve developing in missions. The movement will eventually gain more and more steam, but something else will eventually take its place. This trend is still in its early S stage, and is still developing. It is not entirely evident how far this trend will go, but because it is so widespread, it stands to be significant.

As we begin the next chapter, it will be important to remember that the principles of research and evidence-based decision making should underscore everything we do. We should recognize that our ministries are often isolated from the effects of change, and we need to be intentional about looking for the various changes happening around us. We need to identify and challenge the assumptions we hold which keep us from true innovative thinking.

We will need to stop oversimplifying issues and begin thinking in terms of complex, interrelated systems. We need to look for the potential ripple effects of our actions and recognize the rule of unintended consequences. Finally, we need to remember that all trends, ideas, plans, and initiatives follow a natural cycle of growth and decline. We need to begin experimenting with new ideas long before existing programs fizzle out. Doing so gives these new ideas time to develop so that we are not caught off guard. Waiting too long to try new ideas could be dangerous to our organizations.

CHAPTER 6

SCENARIO PLANNING

"The tribe of Issachar supplied 200 leaders, along with all of their relatives under their command. They kept up-to-date in their understanding of the times and knew what Israel should do." 1 Chronicles 12:32 (ISV)

AN ARRAY OF PLAUSIBLE FUTURES

Aside from occasionally revealing parts of the future to his prophets, God prefers to let it remain uncertain until it finally arrives. If we were prophets, we might look for the one singular future which will occur. For the rest of us, that's not possible. The future contains an infinite number of possibilities which may or may not occur. Instead of trying to find out which specific future might emerge, it's actually better to think of the future in the plural, as an array of plausible futures (Hines and Bishop 2006).

Approaching the future as a plural array of plausible futures does not come easily, especially for Christians. The idea of prophesy or "predicting" the future comes from the idea that only one singular future exists. We ask, "Who is *the one* I will marry?" or "Will she accept Christ?" These are closed ended questions. We assume that it will either rain, or it won't. Such questions limit the scope of our thinking about a wider range of potential futures.

Thinking about the future in plural terms leads to a completely different set of questions (2006). When thinking in the plural, we begin to think about the various forces which bear influence on various future scenarios. Looking at an array of futures, one begins to ask open-ended questions: "What type of person should I marry?" "Under what conditions might she accept Christ?" "What might influence her towards this decision?" "What early indicators could I identify that will help me understand which way she is moving?'

Just because we cannot predict the future doesn't mean we have to live in uncertainty (2006). Focusing on a set of probable futures helps us be ready for a variety of different future scenarios. To help us prepare for these scenarios, we examine the various trends and events bearing influence on the actions and decisions defining the emerging future.

A weather forecaster looks at various weather patterns and how they will interact; then a forecast is developed for the next few days and weeks (2006). As weather trends develop and change, the forecaster updates his forecast to match new emerging information. Over time, the weather forecaster develops his skills and begins to understand to which types of information he must play close attention and what information he can ignore. The better the forecaster is at understanding such trends, the more accurate his forecasts will be. Short term forecasts are often more accurate than long term forecasts, and sometimes unforeseen events steer forecasts in new directions. Good forecasters know how to spot outside influences early.

Weather forecasters don't make *predictions;* they make *forecasts.* Predictions are precise, exact statements about what the future will be. Forecasts, however, provide just enough meaningful information to help us make better decisions about our day: should I take an umbrella, should I delay my beach vacation, or should buy a snow-blower? Forecasts acknowledge the unknown: if the tropical storm continues in this direction, we will have wind and rain. But, in another scenario, it will move out to sea, and we'll have sun. Forecasts provide enough information to help people prepare for either scenario.

We too, should think about the future in terms of forecasting, not predicting. We track various trends and events impacting the environment surrounding our ministries in order to paint various probable scenarios impacting the future of our ministry. If we had a constant flow of accurate predictions from a prophet, we could prepare specifically for one pre-determined scenario. Forecasts give us information about the future that empower us to take meaningful action today amid informed uncertainty (Saffo 2007).

Viewing the future as an unfolding array is an essential part of scenario planning (Hines and Bishop 2006). As we learn about trends, events, and potential wild-card scenarios influencing our world, we narrow down all the possible futures into an array of plausible futures. We use this information to write detailed scenarios about the future.

ARRAY FOR PLAUSIBLE FUTURES

In the process of exploring these scenarios, we learn ways in which we can influence the future as it emerges (2006). As such, the goal is not to create a scenario which perfectly reflects the future. These scenarios are not graded by how closely they reflect the future. Scenarios are valuable for their ability to create meaningful dialogue regarding the future. A good scenario simply helps us think about the future in a way that helps us become like the leaders of Issachar, understanding the times and knowing what to do as a result.

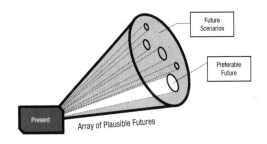

Adopted from Hines and Bishop, *Thinking about the Future*, 2006.

As we gain a deeper understanding about what the future is likely to look like, we can begin to explore another type of scenario, one describing our most *preferred future*. What do we want the future to look like? How can we make sure we get to that future? How can we influence our environment to ensure that our most *preferred future* is the one that emerges?

ENVIRONMENT SCANNING AND SCAN HITS

The first part of scenario creation is environment scanning. A ship's captain constantly scans his horizon, monitoring the environment above, below, forward, behind, left, and right for anything that might influence the journey (2006). Failure to identify changes in the environment could lead to catastrophic problems. Such was the fate of the Costa Concordia in 2014, which ran aground in Italy, killing thirty-four people. The accident was blamed on the captain, who, interestingly was accused of having stopped scanning his environment (Dinmore, Segreti, & deSabata 2012). Accurate scanning alerts us to necessary changes of course.

Environment scanning is simply the process of gathering information about our local and global surroundings which may influence the future, including the future of our organizations or the environment in which our organization exists (Bishop 2005). It takes note of any changes which have the potential to impact the organization and its domain (Burke 2011). Thus, when scanning, it is important to look for changes as broadly as possible. Strategists often use the "STEEP" framework as a guideline. STEEP stands for changes in the Social, Technical, Environmental, Economic and Political domains (Bishop 2005). Some companies add Demographic as a separate category, while others simply record this in the social category. I have found using it as a separate category aids when discussing changes in people groups. Ministries generally add the Religious category as well.

Scanning Domains

Keeping these seven domains in mind, we begin looking for events, issues, ideas, constants, cycles, plans, emerging trends, and projections which might impact the domain in which our organization operates. The sources for this information are practically limitless. They include research, the Internet, magazines, books, conversations, the news, observations, experience, or any number of other sources.

SCANNING DOMAINS:

- Social
- Technical
- Environmental
- Economic
- Political
- Demographic
- Religious

When notable information is found, it is called a scan hit (2005). Scan hits should be recorded for future reference, creating a library of potential influences on the future. It should be noted that scan hits lose their importance with time. Emphasis should be placed upon developing a continuous stream of new scan hits.

When recording the scan hit, the following information should be included: a title for the scan hit, the author or source providing the hit and the date it was recorded, a category indicating the domain to which the hit belongs, the source of the hit (the website, periodical, news broadcast, etc.), a detailed description of the information found, and the perceived potential effect on the future, implications which should be analyzed, and how it could influence the organization or its domain. Next, the hit should be rated on a zero to five scale in terms of the perceived impact on the future and plausibility of the issue or event actually occurring. The hit's timeliness indicates how soon the information would create an impact and its potential to create true innovation.

It should be noted that choosing the specific category (STEEP, D, R) as well as the specific rating for impact, plausibility, timeliness, and innovation will be largely subjective according to your own perspective. If you find a scan hit that looks particularly interesting, you may want to get a broader perspective on the specific ratings. As you find more scan hits, you will begin to create your own system of evaluation. The categorization and rating systems exist primarily as ways to organize and evaluate the importance of your growing library of scan hits. Sharing scan hits is an important part of the process; it empowers the process of discussing potential impacts on the future, as well as opportunities to be seized today.

Scan Hit Contents

For instance, I came across a paper by the Center for the Study of Global Christianity at Gordon Conwell Theological Seminary (2013). This report was the source for a number of scan hits utilized in identifying mega-trends in the first chapters of this book. One scan hit was created about an emerging issue: most native missionaries sent out from the Global South are simply reaching their own country's diaspora peoples (overseas migrant workers) and not reaching native populations. That is, South American missionaries serving in Africa, for the most part, bring South Americans living in Africa, not native Africans, to Christ.

SCAN HIT:
(Trends, Events, Issues, Decisions, etc.)

Title:
Author/Date:
Category: S / T / E / E / P / D / R
Source:
Description:

Potential effect on future and implications:

Impact (Scale 0-5):   Plausibility (Scale 0-5):
Timeliness (Scale 0-5):   Innovation (Scale 0-5):

All the information collected regarding mega-trends in this book came from scan hits collected over a three year period. It takes time and effort to build a useful repository of scan hits which will provide you with meaningful information about the future. With time, anyone can create a rich and meaningful resource of information. Using mega-trends such as the ones listed in this book are a great source for starting your repository. The more trends you track, the higher quality future scenarios you will be able to create.

Many who become serious about collecting scan hits keep a notepad with them at all times. When one begins thinking about how information they glean has the potential to influence the future, they begin paying closer attention to casual conversations, the evening news, conferences, Sunday sermons, etc. I keep my scan hits in a digital notebook, accessible from my phone, computer, and tablet. Apps like Evernote and OneNote allow you to capture webpages, images, audio, etc. from any of your digital devices.

The scan hit from Gordon Conwell was recorded as follows:

Scan Hit Sample 1

While reading the news, I found an article referencing a research study conducted by Price Waterhouse Coopers (2013). As I thought about the implications of the article, the information seemed particularly relevant. A quick Internet search produced the original research report on PWC's corporate website. I saved the research article and entered the following information as a scan hit:

SCAN HIT:
(Trends, Events, Issues, Decisions, etc.)

Title: Christianity in its global context, 1970-2020

Author/Date: Gordon Conwell, Center for the Study of Global Christianity, 2013

Category: S/T/E/E/P/D/ (**R**) Religious

Source: http://www.gordonconwell.com/netcommunity/CSGCResources/Christianityin-itsGlobalContext.pdf

Description: Missionaries sent out from the Global South predominately reach their own diaspora peoples (same culture international migrant workers), not the native peoples of the target countries. Overall cross cultural effectiveness remains low.

Potential effect on future and implications: Without outside help, these movements will struggle to reach the indigenous population. Opportunity exists for mission agencies of the Global North to come alongside and equip. With the size and scope of this emerging mission movement, there is tremendous opportunity for the Global North to influence the south, provided it doesn't revert to paternalism and control.

Impact (Scale 0-5): 3   Plausibility (Scale 0-5): 5
Timeliness (Scale 0-5): 5   Innovation (Scale 0-5): 3

Sample Scan Hit 2

It is important to build a large library of scan hits (Bishop, 2005). Read the news with an appreciation of how these daily events might impact the future. Keep emails which discuss emerging technologies. Take notes from conversations and conferences. Pay attention to anything which might disrupt the future in new and interesting ways. The more information you have the more informed you'll become about the future.

SCAN HIT:
(Trends, Events, Issues, Decisions, etc.)

Title: Talent Mobility 2020

Author/Date: PriceWaterhouseCoopers, 2013

Category: S/T/E/(E)/P/(D)/R Economic, Demographic

Source: http://pwc.com/managingpeople2020

Description: International job posts are likely to double by the year 2020

Potential effect on future and implications: Corresponds with another scan hit that large numbers of Christians are taking international job posts and live out a missional lifestyle reaching local peoples. More jobs = more opportunity. What an opportunity to create a self-funded mission force! What's needed for them to be effective? Who will train and equip them? Will it be an informal entwork? YouTube based? Or would they want regional conferences? Is it an opportunity for a new type of mission organization?

Impact (Scale 0-5): 5   Plausibility (Scale 0-5): 4
Timeliness (Scale 0-5): 5   Innovation (Scale 0-5): 5

When collecting scan hits it is important to be aware of our own internal biases (Morlidge and Player 2010). Some biases come from a natural tendency to seek only that information which confirms what we already believe. To counteract this bias, actively seek out information contrary to your own assumptions about the future. Another form of bias happens when we fail to logically think through consequences. When you find an interesting scan hit, talk to others in other fields or industries, about their opinion on the issue. Bias can also happen when we make judgments on irrelevant, outdated, or incorrect information. To counteract this bias, seek to confirm the information in your scan hits. Notice, when I read an article referencing research by PWC, I went directly to PWC and sought the original research. You'd be amazed how often research studies are twisted, misrepresented, and misinterpreted into completely unrelated applications. So, as much as possible, seek out the original research. Also be aware of any potential biases of the researchers. Be careful, however, not to throw out a scan hit just because it doesn't conform to your preconceived ideas.

Now is the time to get started. Put down this book and begin reading the news, journals, magazines, company reports, etc. Look for emerging trends, significant events, new issues, or decisions which may have an impact on the future. Begin asking how the information in these articles could influence the future of ministry. Record the article and create a scan hit according to the process above. Try creating twenty unique scan hits. You may want to a digital notebook to record these hits. Keep your notepad, phone, or tablet with you as you read or watch the news every day. If you work in a team, get your teammates to join with you. Use the information gained to spark conversations about the future. Some of these notebooks can be shared with a team quite easily.

The rest of this book will be much more meaningful if you take the time to record twenty scan hits now. You will need this information to understand and practice the next step.

IMPACT MAPS

Once you have a growing collection of emerging trends, events, issues, and decisions, it is important to begin thinking about how they might interact (Glenn 2009). The impact map is one of the most commonly used tools to begin the process of formulating scenarios. Impact maps are used by government agencies, salmon farmers, economic planners, educators, the tourism industry, and especially the oil and gas industries. This visual process helps us explore ripple effects of various changes. You can do this by yourself, but it is better to work with others, as it will lead to more interesting and higher quality results. You'll need a felt pen and a large sheet of paper.

In the center of the paper, write the name of a trend, event, or issue and draw a circle around it. Next, draw four or five short spokes from the center of the circle, in all directions. Each spoke will end with its own circle, representing ripple effects, or secondary repercussions.

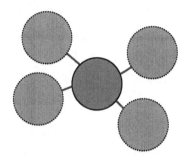

Think about what might happen because of this trend, issue, or event. If a particular trend develops, what might happen as a result? Write those in the circles representing the secondary repercussions.

We could use the increasingly plausible idea that a company mass produces self-driving cars. This is a great opportunity to use an impact map and see the repercussions this might create. Begin by naming the circle in the middle of the paper "Self-driving car." Draw the spokes out and begin thinking, "What repercussions could this create?" For one, we might eventually be able to program our cars to take our kids to soccer practice. Further brainstorming, we think how police stations could automatically re-route cars around accidents or to reduce congestion. On the negative side, software glitches create terrible traffic accidents. Lastly, someone jokingly wonders if people might be required to register their car with restaurants if they order alcohol. Through an app, bartenders allow patrons to program a destination, but lock them out from personally driving the car until they've had enough time to sober up. The impact map begins to look like this:

Impact Map for Self-Driving Car

Now, from the outer circles, draw more lines and circles to represent third level impacts. Think about the repercussions of your second level circles. What will happen if parents let their cars take their kids to soccer practice? What might be the repercussions if traffic is controlled remotely by the police? What happens if software glitches become a significant source of traffic accidents?

After you identify third level impacts, continue into fourth level (and occasionally, fifth level) repercussions. The most creative ideas generally begin to emerge at the third and fourth levels. These also take the most time and energy to brainstorm. Be careful to check your assumptions. What factors constrain your thinking? Continue until you or the team feels it understands the full repercussions of an event or issue.

Back to our example: if self-driving cars take kids to soccer practice, soccer moms and dads would need a way to ensure their kids actually got out of the car safely. Phone apps would need to track both the car and their kids. Not having to drive their kids, soccer parents might find the time to take another job or start a new business. If they did this, they might need yet another car. This result would mean greater traffic congestion and a significant increase in consumption of fossil fuels. Gas prices could increase as a result. The impact map might look like this:

Impact Map for Self-driving Car

During the process, you may find links between multiple different repercussions. Simply connect the lines as needed. In the beginning, this process will go quickly. Use systems thinking to consider how issues may impact various social systems, ministries, societies, or even business and government.

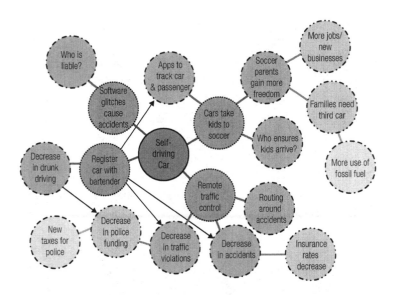

Continuously challenge your own assumptions. What do you assume to be true—which may turn out to be false? Think about the process of creative destruction: what new opportunities will develop? What will become obsolete? Move beyond surface issues and try to examine issues on a deeper level. Where might more research be required?

You may need to edit your impact map to make it more realistic (2009). It is easy to jump to conclusions. One event is never enough to produce the impacts you identify. For instance, it will take much more than the production of a self-driving car before soccer parents would legally (or safely) send their children to soccer practice alone. It is important to ask, "What else is necessary for this scenario to realistically emerge?" "What issues need to be solved?" "How might we be able to influence the emergence of these various ideas? You may want to remove impacts that are simply too unrealistic (but make a record of what you delete). Think about what early indicators might signal that such an improbable event might actually happen. You may find that some of the craziest ideas lead to some of the best opportunities.

This tool is ideal for helping individuals move from linear cause and effect thinking to nonlinear, complex, network-oriented thinking. We can use this process to track the probable repercussions of various national mission movements, funding scenarios, initiatives, societal trends, etc. The process is best done in a small group environment which produces a diversity of ideas as well as rich discussion (2009).

The power of the impact map is in exploring the repercussions of emerging events, trends, and issues. It helps teams become creative in exploring potential future scenarios and how those scenarios may develop. It is an important part of exploring and preparing for the potential future environment.

Here's another impact map relating to the church. We took the idea of churches refocusing on the Missio Dei, the mission of God (as was noted in the "Changing American Church" section in an earlier chapter):

Impact Map for Missio Dei

What would you add or change in the above impact map? What are further fourth and fifth level repercussions?

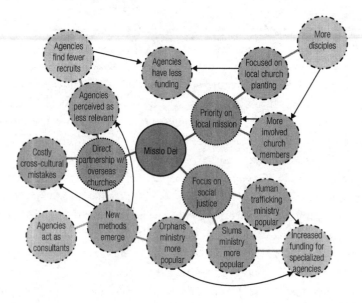

These impact maps are not supposed to represent predictions of the future. Impact maps are designed to help us understand the repercussions of various issues and events. They help us understand what might happen and why. They help us understand how systems operate. Consider, for instance, if someone might have stopped to create an impact map relating to the malnourishment example given before. They could have realized that food subsidies would have created an even larger problem down the road. Or, consider if someone would have taken the time to do this before intervening in the church planting example. If one of the well-meaning Christians would have taken the time to understand what was causing the new house churches to be planted, and create an impact map with included positive and negative repercussions for paying pastors and renting meeting spaces, imagine what could have happened. They could have realized that their actions would disrupt the cascading system behind all the new house churches. They could have realized that their actions had the potential to stop a greater work of God.

Our goal is never to create accurate predictions. The goal is to find leverage points where we should, and should not exert influence on the future. The goal is to find opportunities for positive engagement and avoid opportunities for negative repercussions. The goal is to understand forces and trends so that we might help an entirely different future to emerge; one that is beneficial to us and the objectives we desire to achieve.

After you have gathered a significant number of scan hits, look for the most interesting trends or ideas. Look for ones which might have a high degree of impact on the future. Then begin creating impact maps based upon that scan hit. Repeat the process with multiple trends to explore different potential futures. The information gained from this exercise should be rich and meaningful. We will use this information as we begin creating scenarios, next.

Before you move on to the next section, put this book down and create two different impact maps. Doing so will provide necessary information for your next step.

SCENARIOS

All that you've learned up to this point will be used to create a number of scenarios, exploring various potential futures. "A scenario is a story with plausible cause and effect links that connects a future condition with the present, while illustrating key decisions, events, and consequences throughout the narrative" (Glenn 2009, 2). These scenarios range from a few paragraphs to a few pages in length. They are not predictions; they are plausible projections of what could happen given the interaction of emerging trends, events, and issues. These scenarios should provide a plausible framework that describes the process in which each scenario would emerge.

Creating scenarios helps us explore three very different images of the future. There are three types of future scenarios: the expected, alternative, and wild-card futures (Gary 2012).

Scenarios regarding the *expected future* explore the future we expect to emerge given the extrapolation of today's major trends and issues. *Alternative future* scenarios explore other plausible futures that could emerge given changes in trends, issues, or events that we observe emerging on the fringes. These scenarios take into account emerging trends and issues that are not yet fully developed but that have the potential to significantly change the future.

The *wild-card future* looks at potential wild-card (surprise) events which have the capacity to significantly disrupt the future. A wild-card event is something that has low probability but would produce radical change. Identifying and tracking potential wild-card events helps us plan for the unexpected.

Scenario planning became popular after the oil crisis of the 1970's (Glenn 2009). Shell Oil, then a relatively small oil company, had written various scenarios for expected, alternate, and wild-card futures within the oil industry. They questioned significant assumptions which everyone else in the industry took for granted. Shell identified several wild-card events which would fundamentally change the way oil was bought and sold in the Middle East. As they developed scenarios, complete with *early indicators* that such a scenario was actually emerging, they made a revelation. One of the wild-card events they identified was much more plausible than anyone was anticipating.

Shell continued normal operations, but also began creating contingency plans just in case the wild-card event might occur. Shell noticed that several early indicators identified in the scenario were actually starting to emerge. No one else in the oil industry was paying attention to these seemingly insignificant events. Then, suddenly everything changed. The largest oil companies were all caught off guard, but Shell was prepared and found itself catapulted into an industry leader. The big companies found themselves playing catch-up to this second tier oil company. Everyone wondered how such a small company could have known such changes were coming. Today, governments and non-profits are using scenario planning to explore the wild-card possibility of the collapse of North Korea. What might happen as a result? What issues would their citizens face? How could missionaries be deployed and used most effectively? What training would they need? This type of planning helps organizations prepare for a variety of future scenarios. Organizations taking the time to plan in this way are poised to take the lead, no matter what situation eventually emerges. These are the organizations that are taking the time to understand the times and know what to do as a result.

The scenarios we write create a framework to think about the future in a logical, methodological way. It helps us understand a number of plausible futures while providing a roadmap, showing how each potential future could develop. The goal of writing scenarios is not to create a perfect prediction, but to help us explore challenges and opportunities. Such information allows us to prepare and create innovative solutions which align us to the future, while helping us shape that future in the process.

J. Glenn, a significant contributor to the development of futures research methodologies, states:

> The purpose of scenarios is to systematically explore, create, and test consistent alternative future environments that encompass the broadest set of future operating conditions that the user might plausibly face. Scenarios can help generate long-term policies, strategies, and plans, which help bring desired and likely future circumstances in closer alignment. While writing the scenarios, the process can also expose ignorance; show that we do not know how to get to a specific future or that it is impossible. Furthermore, they serve to bring assumptions about the field they cover to the foreground and can serve as a tool to discuss, test and maybe re-evaluate these assumptions . . ." (Glenn 2009, 3)

There are a number of different methods for writing scenarios (Glenn 2009). Scenarios can be developed by individuals or by teams through group process.

The first step is to define the scope of the scenario. This involves defining the key variables and driving forces (issues, trends, repercussions, etc.) to be examined. Scenarios should be developed for a variety of different futures, including the expected future, alternative futures, as well as wild-card futures. Doing a quality job of collecting scan hits and developing impact maps will make the process much more informed and purposeful. Research should be utilized wherever possible. The scenario should take into account various stakeholders, including their possible strategies, actions, and reactions to various trend events. For instance: If online free Bibles become the preferred method of Bible reading, how will this impact various stakeholders (publishers, Bible translators, bookstores)? How will they react? What strategies might they employ to protect their businesses?

Setting the horizon time for the scenario is a very important step. The scenario should be set far enough into the future that it causes you to think past current conditions. Things will change. The scenario is developed to help you imagine those changes. Moving into the range of twenty years will help you identify higher and higher level capabilities.

Twenty years ago, I had just learned about the Internet and the World Wide Web, and I wasn't sure if it would ever catch on. I was preparing to buy an expensive film camera (which is now useless!), and I didn't see the point of owning an expensive cell phone. Do you see how much things have changed in these twenty years? It is important to take the time to seriously consider the higher level capabilities that might be available in the future. How will perceptions change? How might forces combine to alter people's opinions on issues? In many cases, fifteen to twenty years should be the minimum time range. In certain fast moving industries, however, a shorter time range is necessary. In other cases, a much longer time range might be preferred. Take the time to consider your timeframe.

Finally, the scenario writer should identify milestones or leading indicators which could indicate whether or not such a future scenario is actually emerging. For instance: if North Korea were to begin to collapse, or open up, what might be some leading indicators? If China were to attempt to annex North Korea as a province, what initial steps might China take to move in this direction? How might China react to the democratization of North Korea? What are the important issues which will emerge in the process? Thinking through these scenarios helps us be prepared no matter what happens.

The following is an example of a scenario; it is an educated guess about the future, written in story form. It explores ministry opportunities in a plausible alternative future taking place in the Middle East. The scenario takes into account the interaction of various trends happening in mission sending, young adults in the American church, growing international positions for expat workers, stakeholders in remote Muslim villages, etc. The scenario is several pages long and explores this plausible future from two different viewpoints, one of which is a plausible first hand story of the changes. The scenario ends with the identification of several leading indicators that this scenario could actually emerge. The story is *written from the perspective of the future, looking back* on various changes which occurred to create the specific future scenario. The scenario also provides insight for mission agencies to consider which might influence the emergence of this future. It also provides mission agencies insight into opportunities and potential roles they may take in an emerging future. *The scenario is not real;* it is a creative glimpse of what could happen, given the convergence of multiple trends and issues. It is written, however, from the standpoint that it is, in fact, real. Furthermore, to make it as real as possible, the scenario is constructed as if it is written in the future, after specific events have taken place. This helps the scenario be as realistic as possible, helping the reader understand the issues and opportunities present.

The scenario is written in the past tense. It is written by some imaginary person, in the future, remembering the events that transpired to get them to this point. The scenarios you write should be written in a similar manner.

Example of a Plausible Scenario

The Development of Christian Mission in the Middle East (year 2030): In the late 2010's young people the American church came alive. New Calvinism flooded into the church bringing a new appreciation for scripture reading and discipleship among the youth. At the same time, Pentecostals developed an army of young church planters. These young adults took the Bible at its word and felt the challenge to put their faith into practice. They were also highly driven towards both self-development and career development. At the same time, a new mission movement was birthed out of American Hispanic churches.

Companies such as Intel, Motorola, AMD, Amazon, Microsoft, Apple, etc. expanded international operations rapidly during this time into China, Indonesia, Vietnam, Russia, Turkey, Nigeria, and Saudi Arabia, to name but a few. These corporations offered accelerated career development packages to anyone willing to take the overseas positions. These positions provided visas, income, cultural training, overseas allowances, etc., making overseas life quite comfortable.

Newly graduated and eager to make their mark on the world, and finding it hard to find promising jobs in the States, young New Calvinist, Pentecostal, and Hispanic believers eagerly took overseas positions. These positions allowed these young Christians to live overseas in a missional lifestyle among non-believers while receiving a salary that could pay off their significant student loans. These individuals gravitated to countries traditionally closed to missionary activity where they could actively put their faith on display in the workplace.

They found their national coworkers to be open to Western ideas. Discussions about differences in their religious beliefs were easy to start. The locals they interacted with were eager to improve their English skills and eagerly talked with their American co-workers about anything. Many of these national co-workers were from small towns located far from the city. Practically every region of the country and every ethnic group were represented in the office. It created a rich working environment.

As these American Christians came back to the US and shared their stories, droves of other young believers began following in their footsteps overseas. Books were written about their experiences. One particular American expat had written a blog, "The Missional Expat," which was published and became a best-selling Christian book. A true movement emerged.

At the same time, missionaries began looking for new inroads to closed societies. Changes in the American church eroded much of mission funding. Out of necessity, missionaries began facing the truth. Their profession must change or die. One innovative organization began focusing on creating missional apps for smart phones. Missionaries began putting their best resources into these apps, including their resources for discipleship, training, and church planting.

Declining resources fueled a need to seek new partners. Missionaries found that businesses, particularly larger Western corporations, enjoyed a certain amount of safety in countries traditionally closed to missionary activity. These businesses were often less monitored by police and clerics than public places where missionaries often engaged in their activities. Evangelism on the street, in the cafes, and in the marketplace was heavily monitored; yet office place evangelism was often overlooked. Indeed, these young millennial expat American Christians were leading many natives to Christ.

In these businesses, entire teams became Christian with little repercussion. The biggest repercussions were not from the police, but management who complained about using business hours for Bible study. Still, since Muslims used some of the conference rooms for prayers, Christians were equally welcome to use other unused conference rooms as long as it did not create a disruption.

A few missionaries began training expats in best practices in mission, including multiplicative discipleship methods. A few organizations caught on to the practice as well. Before long, an army of young expat professionals were helping their national co-workers start home-based Bible studies. Expat churches offered seminars on work/mission integration, which were taught by missionaries and mission organizations. These weekend seminars were well attended. Networks between expat churches grew up overnight for discussing successes and challenges to workplace ministry. It wasn't long before national movements began emerging from their efforts.

In 2026, the organizers of these seminars wrote a book highlighting their methods for starting church planting movements through overseas expat positions. The book became the cornerstone of the expat missional movement. It was entitled, *Missional Expats: Making the Most of Your Overseas Assignment.* Here is an excerpt of one of the transformational stories captured in the book:

Book Excerpt: Our mission team had been seeking inroads to reach these remote Muslims for years. We prayed. We fasted. We desired God to use us to reach this people. Yet we didn't know how, and every door seemed to shut before us. Still we prayed that God would shine his light among this people we so longed to reach.

Then, as we were still trying to secure long term access to the country, it was drawn to our attention that house churches were seemingly materializing across the countryside. Curious to find out why, we initiated a full investigation. We sought, if possible, to find the true number of churches and what was fueling this new movement. What our research found was absolutely astounding.

We hired local Christians as researchers who, at first, found little evidence of these churches. As they were wandering around one village which had supposedly recently seen a number of churches start, they began seeing crude symbols scratched into stones in alleyways. The researchers immediately recognized the symbols as ichthuses, though much more modern in design. One local man, observing that we understood the sign, pulled the team aside and offered them coffee.

The man invited them to his home and told them a story about a young man named Ahmed, who worked at one of the big international conglomerates in the capital city. Ahmed shared a cubicle with an American named Mateo. The two became friends from the moment they met. After six months, there was no subject which they couldn't talk about, especially their respective religions. Ahmed had made it a personal goal to convert Mateo.

About this time, Mateo's best friend was killed by an IED as he was inspecting the construction of pipelines. Ahmed was struck with the fact that Mateo forgave and even prayed God's blessing on those who set the IED. Before long Ahmed became a Christian.

Ahmed kept his faith quietly to himself, until one day, he noticed another employee sitting quietly reading a Bible in the break room. This other employee had a similar experience with an American coworker who had forgiven and even prayed a blessing upon the organizers of a terrorist attack. The two began studying and praying together.

Ahmed and his friend began asking Mateo about church and how new Christians could grow and learn about the Bible. Afraid to use the word "church" Ahmed and his friend started a "club" to talk about Isa (as Jesus is called in the Koran). The Isa club grew rapidly. Soon, every floor of the office had a small Isa club that was meeting after hours.

Ahmed's wife began seeing changes in her husband. He had suddenly started treating her much better than before, and began taking a deeper interest in her wellbeing and interests. Curious (and yet a bit frightened) she finally confronted her husband. Ahmed quietly explained how Isa had changed his heart, from the inside. Ahmed then explained how he and others had formed an Isa club at the office. A few weeks later, Ahmed's wife revealed a secret. She too had secretly become a Christian, but was afraid to tell him.

Ramadan came and Ahmed and his wife went back to their village to celebrate with family. Ahmed's father found a Bible in their suitcase and became furious. At first he did nothing because Ahmed was somewhat a local hero, working in the capital and earning such a high income. But the following year when Ahmed returned again for Ramadan, his father killed him.

That night, Ahmed's father had a dream. Ahmed was standing at the foot of his bed. All Ahmed said was, "I forgive you, father. Isa loves you and wants to forgive you too." The next day, the father openly converted to Christianity, fearlessly proclaiming the message of Isa.

As we finished our coffee, the man said, "Ahmed was my son. Proclaiming Isa, I have nothing to lose. If they kill me, I am merely reunited with my son. No one on this earth can hurt me. God gave me goal to plant a church in every village of my province. Do you know Isa?"

This scenario's leading indicators:

- Growth in expat jobs in closed countries.
- Growth in zeal and focus on discipleship of young believers.
- Young believers rejecting missions for overseas professional placements.
- Muslims becoming Christians while working in foreign conglomerates.
- Expat churches requesting evangelism and cell church training.

The preceding scenario was a creative glimpse written about a probable future based upon a number of emerging trends. This included the New Calvinist movement sweeping through many churches, the likely start of a Hispanic mission movement, the growth of international job postings in closed countries, and the growing trend of young people choosing to live missionally in their careers in otherwise closed nations. Writing scenarios such as this help us wrestle with the issues likely to be faced.

Scenarios also highlight the support structures needed along the way. For instance, when I first wrote this scenario, I recognized that expatriate churches would likely play a vital role in equipping these young professionals to be effective in their witness. I found this to be a particularly good opportunity for agencies to get involved today.

Scenarios are an important aspect of exploring expected, alternative, and wild-card futures (Gary 2012). Developing multiple scenarios allows us to create multiple images of the future based upon the issues and events we see emerging. Scenario planning also highlights opportunities for new innovative ideas. They also help us understand the viability of our ideas or obstacles that might be encountered along the way. Scenarios should spark conversations about innovation, new initiatives, and opportunities that are waiting to be taken. They can revitalize languishing projects and ignite new ones.

One ministry leader had a scan hit discussing how Africa could potentially become a world power in the next forty to fifty years. Along with a large cross-section of African Christians from ministries, universities, and even from the business world, they explored this scenario. They discussed what such a future Africa would look like and what ministries would have to do to be successful in such an environment. The results were transformational for everyone participating.

ASSIGNMENT

Now, for an assignment. Put down this book and look over your scan hits and impact maps. Choose some issues or trends and begin thinking about an expected future, various alternative futures, and wild-card futures. Choose something from the category of alternative futures or wild-card future and begin writing a scenario. Pick a time frame, a minimum of fifteen to twenty years in the future. The further the date you choose, pressure yourself or your team to come up with higher and higher level capabilities. The further you go out, the more unexpected the future will become.

Write the scenario as if you are living in the future. Be sure to write in the past tense, describing how this specific future emerged. Try to write several pages. When you are done, finish by identifying several key indicators which would function as early indicators that such a future was actually emerging. Give your scenario to someone else, and ask for their input, which can be invaluable. You know you've created a good scenario if the person reading it forgets that it's not a real story.

CHAPTER 7

INSTITUTIONALIZING A CULTURE OF INNOVATION

"The whole body, being fitted and held together by what every joint supplies, according to the proper working of each individual part, causes the growth of the body for the building up of itself in love." Ephesians 4:6 (NASB)

The art of innovation lies in using what you've learned through the scenario building process for identifying higher impact opportunities. Peter Drucker wrote, "There are, of course, innovations that spring from a flash of genius. Most innovations, however, especially the successful ones, result from a conscious, purposeful search for innovation opportunities" (Drucker 1985, 3). The tools discussed in previous chapters are some of the most widely used tools to which today's businesses are turning for finding these innovative ideas.

These innovative ideas certainly come from a variety of sources. Drucker talked of this as a "flash of genius." Flashes of genius, however, are hard to come by and are notoriously unpredictable. It's also generally not recommended to rely on one single innovative thinker to find new ideas and opportunities. Such a person will find themselves frustratingly at odds with the larger team.

Instead, businesses institutionalize the innovation process. They create innovation centers based upon these principles. They empower their employees, then reward them for coming up with new ideas.

Bill O'Brien, former vice president at the Southern Baptist Convention Foreign Mission Board (now the International Mission Board), has been helping Christian organizations institutionalize the innovative process ever since he read an article on the subject written by a NASA physicist (World Futures Society 1994; Seipp 2015). The 1994 article described how NASA's Dr. John Andersen used a group process to challenge his teams' assumptions about interplanetary space travel. The result? His team found a new method of space-propulsion that reduced the time for new probes to get to Jupiter, cutting down several years to a just a couple of months.

According to Obrien, the key is to help a group conceptualize a scenario they've developed, far off into the future; then the group is pressed to find higher and higher level capabilities within that scenario. After identifying an idea or opportunity, the group works backwards to today, discussing all the steps necessary to arrive at this new future. O'Brien says this type of scenario planning results in revolutionary ideas for everyone involved: "This is not a way of creating strategic plans, but it is a way of creating new ways of thinking" (Seipp 2015).

Drucker stated, "Purposeful, systematic innovation begins with the analysis of the sources of new opportunities" (Drucker 1985, 7). The goal of innovation is not just to come up with one new idea, but rather to cause the organization to become purposefully systematic in identifying new opportunities. It is a continuous process of attacking strategic drift, by moving beyond it. It's about aiming for where the ball is going to be, rather than where it is now, or was last year. It's becoming like the tribe of Issachar, knowing the times and knowing what to do in response.

The Mission Society was facing its twenty-fifth anniversary. They were proud of their history, but felt an uneasiness (Seipp 2015). Leaders noticed a gap developing between their vision and the deployment of missionaries on the ground. O'Brien was called in to help. A cross-section of leaders and missionaries was assembled in Prague in 2008.

Looking at the trends and challenges developing in their world, Vice President Jim Ramsay realized, "If we don't change, we won't be addressing the key global issues in 10–15 years . . ." But it wasn't just about ministry opportunities. Ramsay said, "We have to rethink how we do everything." They assembled a group: a cross-section of individuals from across the organization. They examined scenarios twenty-five years into the future, and it fundamentally changed everyone who participated. Eight years later, Ramsay says, "Broad organizational shift is [still] happening as a result of that meeting—its fingerprints are all over many aspects of our organization today."

The process of orienting the team to the issues of the future, rather than the issues of today, forever changed the members of the team. Ramsay says that new innovative ideas still continue to emerge. As O'Brien said, it's a new way of thinking. It changes people.

The goal is to embed these new ways of thinking into the organization's culture. This is not a one-time activity, but a living process. Each change we encounter is an opportunity for us to use the creativity God gave us to impact our world for Him and His glory. The innovation process must be kept alive. To create such a culture, we begin by focusing on spiritual leadership.

SPIRITUAL LEADERSHIP

Spiritual leadership "reframe(s) our relationships with others, appreciating them with dignity and love." (Oster 2011, Kindle location 78) The Bible describes this type of love as "agapao" love (Winston 2002). It seeks the best for others as described in the beatitudes. Jesus is the ultimate example of this love. He worked for people's best interests; not just their spoken needs, or their surface problems.

According to Oswald Sanders, this kind of spirituality comes from authentically living out the values of discipline, vision, wisdom, decision, courage, humility, integrity, sincerity, and humor (Sanders 1967). When corporations lack these values, they become crippled, difficult places in which to work (Mitroff and Denton 1999). Teams working in an atmosphere starved of these values stagnate (Winston 2002; Sanders 1967). Moreover, innovation won't thrive in such an environment either (Oster 2011).

Agapao love focuses on truly loving God and others. This kind of love builds maturity, both in the giver and the receiver. All it takes is for one individual consistently living out this kind of love to radically transform toxic relationships into healthy ones (Clinton and Sibcy 2006). It transforms ordinary teams into high performance teams (MacMillan 2001).

It should be noted that just because an organization performs *spiritual ministry* does not necessarily mean the organization dynamics are also *spiritual* (Sanders 1967). Ministry organizations can easily be devoid of wisdom, courage, love, trust, vision, or other values. An environment of micro-management and distrust will stymie innovation and individual commitment. We have all heard stories of churches led by overbearing pastors, leaving no space for individual soul expression. Though these organizations may be made up of spiritual people, the dynamics are anything but spiritual. It also doesn't matter if the senior leadership team thinks these present in the organization. Leaders may need to invite a few of their individuals out for coffee, and ask them how they perceive the core values of the organization. It may be that some teams model these values well, while others have become toxic.

There is not one "correct" set of values that will transform your organization into a spiritual organization (Mitroff & Denton 1999). Yet, it only takes a few of these values to completely transform the dynamics. The most important factor is that these values are modeled at the top, by the senior leadership (Daft 2008).

Incorporating spiritual values into organizational dynamics will enrich the soil that innovation needs in order to take root and begin growing (Mitroff & Denton 1999). These values also help organizations from calcifying. When organizations become rigid, they quit adapting to external changes. Energy is required to keep our organizations from succumbing to entropy. Just as we do, our organizations need times of renewal. It keeps them fresh and alert to what God desires to do in our changing world.

When organizations are supportive of innovation they adapt faster to their changing environment. Innovation enhances the resilience, or adaptive capacity, of organizations (Holling 2001). It keeps our organizations from becoming a boiling frog. True resilience includes the ability to know when to change and adjust. There is only one thing to which we may hold unswervingly, and that is the gospel of Jesus Christ. God left much of the specific methodology up to us as an expression of the creativity he gave to us.

When the gospel came to Antioch, it was presented with a host of new and different conditions. Peter and the disciples in Jerusalem approached the situation with rigidity. Paul, however, approached the situation with innovation. It created a tense situation resulting in the leadership in Jerusalem having to wrestle through some very difficult and fundamental questions regarding change. Imagine what the church might be like today if Peter and the other apostles had remained rigid on a purely Jewish expression of the Gospel?

Leadership science has changed significantly over time. A hundred years ago, when the environment was changing at a much slower pace, organizations functioned much like factories. The focus was on developing assembly lines with high efficiency. Centralized, hierarchical, and bureaucratic leadership structures supported the standardization of actions which rarely changed. Levels of bureaucracy helped ensure that change happened in a precise manner, where each minute change was understood for its impact on each other area of the manufacturing process. This kept efficiency at its peak.

Today's environment is very different, and it requires a different type of leadership. Having levels of bureaucracy is too rigid to respond to the rapid, daily changes we face. By the time a decision travels up and down each level of command, it's already too late. Strategic drift has widened into a gulf.

To keep up with the changes, organizations have shed layers of management in favor of adaptive structures that can learn and react quickly with a greater degree of autonomy (Daft 2003). As a result, organizations look much flatter. Teams are empowered to make quick decisions, but they must also be able to defend their choices.

The removal of management layers left a hole in the organization (Daft and Lane 2008). To fill the void created by removing layers of management, employees need clearly defined tasks, the empowerment to fulfill those tasks, and accountability to outcomes. Management relationships have to be replaced with team cohesiveness. Tight structure provided by hierarchy was significantly relaxed, and it was found that an atmosphere of professionalism kept the organization from sliding into chaos. On-going training improved the skillset of the workers and contributed to the professionalism, holding the structure together. All these became known as the necessary substitutes for layers of bureaucratic management. When used together, we've found organizations perform much more efficiently than under tight bureaucracy. This leads us to the issue of organizational cultures which promote innovation.

Innovation doesn't just happen. As leaders create space for organizational members to be creative and take reasonable risks, they must foster a culture of innovation. Supporting innovative thinking while stifling the implementation of new ideas will shut down creative ideas and create frustration. Creating an innovative culture happens as leaders reproduce spiritual values in and through other leaders and teams. This takes significant time and effort.

Teams need faith-based stretch goals, to help them reach far beyond their natural abilities, so that innovation is necessary to break through their assumptions about what is possible. All unnecessary obstacles to implementing new solutions need to be removed, while they are encouraged to try multiple small experiments. New ideas should be tried quickly with a value placed upon new insights to be gained. Each failure is a learning opportunity, but failures should come quickly. Keeping innovation experiments small keeps failures from taking down the entire organization, or entire teams in the process.

ORGANIZATIONAL LEARNING

Each team and team leader should promote an intense curiosity among teams where members are encouraged to learn everything they can from other industries and disciplines. This turns teams into "learning factories." This cannot happen in an environment where information is protected and controlled. Organizations have found that as they open up the complete sharing of all organizational data; individuals begin to understand the complex issues being faced. Oster says this about the link between innovation and organizational learning:

> Innovative people and organizations are "learning factories." They consistently capitalize on their God-given talent to explore, learn, and retain new concepts . . . Corporate leadership supports multiple forms of institutional learning and builds systems into place where new information is embraced instead of feared . . . Innovation leaders continually remove physical and organizational barriers that hinder information sharing, and are on the lookout for "sacred cows" and "silos" that hinder the flow of information. (Oster 2011, Kindle Locations 712–23)

Diversity is an important part of organizational learning. Diversity brings people with different perspectives together creating a complexity of thought which has been shown to increase organizational performance, creativity, and innovation (Daft 2008, 332). When people are of the same income level, race, marital status, background, age, etc., they tend to think alike. Religious organizations tend to attract people with similar worldviews and theological views. While conformity may make some working environments easier, it tends to narrow the boundaries of our creative thinking. Even though mission organizations work in a wide diversity of cultures, it is highly possible that the organization itself has very little diversity. Think about the actual diversity that exists among your own leadership structure and on specific teams within your organization. Putting aside the places your people work, how diverse are you, really?

Increasing diversity broadens the breadth of experience and learning from which we may draw. Actively look for people with different backgrounds and experience. Embracing diversity, however, will mean increasing friction within your teams (Daft 2008; Oster 2011). Many Christians seem to have a view that interpersonal, or team friction is somehow unspiritual. If there's no friction, people are all thinking the same way. Productive, positive friction shows you're learning and wrestling with new and creative ideas. Rather than eliminating friction, teams need the skills to work with differing viewpoints in a productive and unthreatening manner (Senge 2006). They need the skills to deal with friction in a healthy way. Too little diversity leads to constrained thinking. Too much diversity leads to dysfunction. Developing a productive amount of diversity is a challenging endeavor. Individuals have a psychological need to fit in on a team (Kristof-Brown et al 2005). Hence, if you have too much diversity, people will shut down, feeling they will never be able to work together. Productive diversity takes time to develop. Every team should understand they'll need to work through Tuckman's developmental stages of forming, storming, norming and performing (Tuckman 1965). After the group forms, they eventually begin storm as they bump into each other's diversity of thought and skill. Here they have the opportunity to learn how to work with each other's differences. Hopefully, people realize that God created us differently in order to fill in each other's gaps of skills and abilities (Werbel & Demarie 2001). If they successfully work through the storming phase, they'll move below the surface, appreciating what each member adds to the team, and eventually launch to high levels of effective performance. But if they cannot get through the storming phase, team members will simply work with each other at a relatively unproductive surface level.

Ephesians 3 and 4 show us how God created his church for diversity. God purposefully placed Gentiles together with the Jews, living stone by living stone, laid next to each other into the temple of God. Paul says he did this in order to display God's manifold (which means diverse!) wisdom. Later, we're told we become mature as we appreciate and make space for the variety of each other's gifts (Eph 4:7–13). We're told that when we walk this way, we walk in love with one another (Eph 4:15).

Paul continues by comparing this diversity to a human body, in which unique parts all work together the way God intended (Eph 4:16). The Gentiles, however, by choosing to live in discord rather than accept diversity, shows that their hearts are darkened and their minds are ignorant (Eph 4:17–18). Paul urges his readers to throw away the old self and walk in this new way, appreciating our diversity which we learn through Christ (Eph 4:20).

DIALOGUE

Some people believe that in order to become a smarter organization, all one needs is smarter people. But just because an organization employs a large number of geniuses doesn't mean the organization is smart (Senge 2006). In fact, in many cases, the higher the collective IQ of an organization, the more dysfunctional the organization becomes. Place the world's brightest economist, psychologist, ecologist, and the world's brightest business mind together in the same room and ask them to solve the world's hunger problem. Odds are they couldn't agree on anything. Goleman (2002) states that when it comes to working together, emotional intelligence is much more important than IQ. The one doesn't necessarily correlate to the other, either. This is why Senge believes that the organizational IQ is generally much lower than the average IQ of the individuals making up that organization. It all depends on whether you are able to get these people to work together effectively. If you can make that happen, it is possible for the organization to operate at a much higher IQ than its member's average. A lot of this relates to the art of dialogue (Senge 2006).

Organizations with high IQ's are called learning organizations. They get their power from their ability to learn more about their environment and collectively process that learning into targeted, innovative action. Learning happens through a skill called dialogue, in which individuals learn to explore new and different ideas from many angles in a non-threatening way. Individuals hold their own judgments loosely, placing a greater value on meaningful group interaction.

Best-selling author and speaker, Senge, states that most business schools place too high of a value on developing student's debate skills, where the emphasis is on presenting and defending ideas (2006). "The usual Western approach to problem-solving or improvement is to attack and criticize, then look for an alternative. This analytical approach does not always lead to creative or fruitful solutions" (Hines and Bishop 2006, 50).

The problem is that debate skills start working against people as they advance through organizational ranks. Eventually, the issues they face become more complex than for what their own personal experience has prepared them (Senge 2006). In essence, they start debating and defending strategies which are beyond their own knowledge and experience. When individuals get to these higher levels, the skills they need are not debating and defending, but the ability to spur creative dialogue and work with the group processes to let new creative solutions emerge.

It's like the findings of Lausanne, 1974: missionaries placed too much focus on proclamation, and not enough time asking questions and helping people wrestle through difficult issues as a part of the discipleship process. Theological schools may be placing too much focus on teaching people how to "teach" theological truth, rather than helping seminary students learn how to help individuals wrestle through the application of spiritual values into their own lives.

Dialogue is one of the top skills needed to navigate the complex future environment. As problems become increasingly complex, we have to learn to release the collective knowledge and experience residing in our teams (Senge 2006). Answers won't come from the top. Debating and arguing about ideas doesn't work. Debates assume the opponent must be won over to a correct point of view. It assumes one person is right and the other is wrong. Dialogue, however, assumes that the answer resides in the collective wisdom of the team. It assumes teammates can, and need to, learn from one another. Differing viewpoints are not opportunities to win someone over; they are opportunities to learn something new. Dialogue has a goal of creating a "shared reality" (Hackman and Johnson 2009, 6). Researchers Reverend & Tannenbaum state, "there is this magical thing in an organization, or in a team, or a group, where you get unrestricted interaction, unrestricted dialogue, and this synergy happening that results in more productivity, and satisfaction, and seemingly magical levels of output from a team . . . The challenge, of course, is in learning to appreciate differences in interpretation without feeling pressured to either demonize the other or strive for complete agreement" (1992, 48).

The result of this kind of dialogue is transformational. Yet for this to happen, organizational goals and group effectiveness have to become more important than any one individual's personal aspirations (Senge, Roberts, Ross, Smith, & Kleiner 1994). The real learning happens as we recognize our assumptions and willingly open them up to others to be probed and explored. Initially, this may feel threatening, but when teammates and organizational members begin placing organizational outcomes above their own ego, true synergy becomes possible.

MIT credits its tremendous successes in creating a long history of technological innovations to this type of dialogue, which they say "mines" the collective intelligence of their people. Imagine the world's smartest PhDs working together, not fighting over who has the better idea, or who gets credit for a breakthrough, but approaching every conversation as an opportunity to learn and build upon each other's ideas. Imagine the depth of maturity this requires.

MIT may think it stumbled upon something revolutionary, but the idea is entirely Biblical. Paul wrote something similar. "Each of you should be concerned not only about your own interests, but about the interests of others as well. You should have the same attitude toward one another that Christ Jesus had, who though he existed in the form of God did not regard equality with God as something to be grasped, but emptied himself by taking on the form of a slave, by looking like other men, and by sharing in human nature. He humbled himself . . ." (Phil 2:3–8, NET). Dialogue requires an atmosphere of humility, especially if individuals are to present their ideas to be challenged and questioned by others. It also requires authenticity where people learn to clearly speak the truth without fear (Eph 4:15).

It requires love, as people examine and challenge the ideas of others in a way that honors our love towards God and our coworkers (Luke 6:31).

Creating an environment in which communication supports creative and innovative ideas is difficult work. It's not about you having a good idea. Focusing too much on your own perspective creates a closed, unfriendly atmosphere (Rubin, Pruitt, and Kim 1994). Alternatively, it's not about complete blindly yielding to others either. Placing all the emphasis on others' ideas ignores the inherent value of your own ideas. And, interestingly, it's not about compromise. Too often compromises result in neither party feeling completely satisfied with the outcome. Rarely will any of these methods of working together lead to an innovative solution.

The secret of this type of rich communication lies in the ability to maintain a high concern for others, while concurrently maintaining a high degree of concern for your own perspective as well. This takes much more time and energy than developing a compromise. To do this, each individual must seek to understand each other individual's world—as it is understood by them (Eisenberg, Goodall, and Trethewey 2010). This requires much deeper communication that surface talk. Its power lies in acknowledging the intrinsic value arising from the diversity of our experiences.

This is the goal of Ephesians 4 diversity: that our conversations become creative processes through deep collaborative interaction emerges. When we get to this place, no individual is carrying an agenda other than to achieve team goals in the best way possible. Deep collaborative interaction doesn't result in compromise, it results in synergistic breakthrough thinking.

In this chapter we talked about some of the essentials necessary to institutionalize a culture of innovation. It begins with developing spiritual organizations led by spiritual leadership. Leaders should model *agapao* love, seeking the best for each individual. We discussed the values necessary to create cultures that support innovation. Next, we discussed orienting our organizations toward continual learning to create organizations with high IQ's. Lastly, we discussed the core skill of dialogue that unleashes the collective experience in teams.

CHAPTER 8

GETTING STARTED

"Go forth . . . to the land I will show you." Genesis 12:1

"Have I not commanded you? Be strong and courageous . . . for the LORD your God is with you wherever you go." Joshua 1:9 (NASB)

THE FOLLY OF GOING "ALL-IN"

When people think of innovators, they often think of big names like Steve Jobs, Thomas Edison, Leonardo da Vinci, or Henry Ford. They think innovators are people that somehow create amazing, game-changing inventions. Interestingly, most innovations are not massive leaps forward.

Ecclesiastes 1 says, "There is nothing new under the sun." It's an interesting verse to quote in a book on innovation. Yet, significant innovations are not something entirely new. Instead, it's the integration and application of knowledge from other fields or industries and finding ways to apply it into your own. For instance, the Wright brothers were experienced glider makers, and although they were focused on the skies, they watched advances in other industries, hoping to find something they could adapt into their glider designs. They incorporated knowledge they learned in their bicycle shop into their designs for controlling their aircraft. While others were focusing on utilizing heavier more powerful engines in their attempts at aviation, the Write brothers were paying attention to smaller gasoline engines were being produced. They paid attention to advances in light-weight metals, and all this gave the Wright brothers an idea. If they could make an engine light enough, they could simply attach it to their glider, making a powered aircraft. The rest is history. Powered flight was simply the result of combining advances from multiple different industries.

Innovators are constantly learning from other fields, looking for anything which might be able to be applied in their own area. Most innovation isn't necessarily a massive leap forward. It starts small. Taking lots of small steps with medium- to low-risk ideas is much more effective than attempting one big, high-risk idea (Hines and Bishop 2006). Placing tremendous effort into one large-scale, high-risk, innovative idea unnecessarily puts the organization, its people, its time, and its finances at risk. Lessons learned from small scale experiments, on the other hand, provide information which flows back into the innovation processes and strengthens future innovation attempts. Successive small experiments build organizational learning and resilience (Hamel and Välikangas 2003). Experimentation on the small scale, on the other hand, feeds the overall process of innovation. When you start putting together all these smaller innovations, the result is much bigger than the sum of the parts.

It turns out most attempts to implement large organizational changes fail, regardless of the usefulness or benefit of the change (Burke 2011). Big reorganizations often don't produce the intended results. Even though the structure changes, under the surface, people tend to revert to the old way. The reason? People don't like being forced to change. Large scale changes create unnecessary resistance (backlash). It takes a lot of time to learn new things, form new habits, and take big risks. Remember our discussion earlier about balancing systems which are resistant to change? Humans seek balance, and they push back on things which disrupt that balance. Forcing large changes on people probably isn't going to end well.

I imagine everyone has experienced this at one time or another: you come up with a great idea, which if people simply adopted, could save them a significant amount of time and money. But no one wants to try this new idea. Inventors are surprised when they meet resistance to their plans. Ministry leaders mistakenly blame the devil for people rejecting changes, which hold the ministry back from reaching its full potential. Unfortunately, the devil often gets more credit than he deserves.

So, what is happening?

First, human systems are complex (Sanders 1998). One plus one rarely equals two; sometimes one plus one equals zero, and sometimes one plus one produces synergy, equaling three, or eight or much more. You cannot assume that if you do A first, and then B, that you'll get C. Linear logic doesn't work with people. Direct, intentional attempts to change the way people interact produces resistance (Burke 2011). Pushing harder creates greater resistance to change. If you force changes through, you often end up with unintended consequences. The larger the change, the greater the resistance.

Change happens best on the small scale (2011). Except for a very small percentage of the human race who seem to love trying new things, people generally want to observe something first before trying it out themselves. If they see how changes have helped someone else, they are much more likely to try it themselves. As more people try it for themselves, still others are watching and growing in their willingness to give it a try. In this way, small scale changes are gradually multiplied up through the organization. It's like planting a garden. You don't start by transplanting mature cabbages, beans, and carrots. You start small, by seeding, watering, and tending to growth. This is the point of the mustard seed parable in Matthew 13:31.

We have all heard the saying, "success breeds success." While some people enjoy trying new things, most people like safety and stability. They want assurance that the time and energy required will be worth the result. By going all in, or going too big too fast, we often end up with unintended consequences. Many times, we end up shooting ourselves in the foot.

One mission group wanted to get their church planting book into the hands of each and every national pastor. They literally printed hundreds of thousands of books. While the book did create initial excitement, it largely failed to have a lasting impact. It was later described as a flash in a pan. Big sparks, but nothing followed. It's not that the book's strategies weren't any good; they were excellent. These practices were based on research and the best practices in the fastest growing churches. The problem came when national pastors tried these practices themselves. One by one, these national pastors tried to make sudden, big changes in their congregations. They couldn't understand why they met with such resistance. Maybe someone should have suggested they start small instead. When they didn't see the same results reflected in the book, they gave up quickly. They blamed the principles for not being relevant to their culture. They blamed the missionaries for failing to contextualize the content. They blamed the devil for thwarting their plans. Even a decade later, I can mention this book to local pastors and get an almost immediate response: "I tried that. It didn't work."

Aiming too high can create a lot of excitement, but it often produces little lasting change. It's often better to take the time to see changes take root in small groups. As you learn from small experiments, take what you've learned and gradually multiply those changes up through the organization or social system. If the changes are worth their while, a small breeze can result in a hurricane of change down the road. If the changes weren't worth their while, at least you didn't waste everyone's time and energy.

The Lausanne Conference highlighted this problem in another context. Country-wide "evangelism crusades" were failing to disciple the nations. In essence, these country-wide evangelism movements, were aiming too high, and were largely failing to change individual lives. The keys to deeper and wider transformational change were found by going slower and starting smaller. Country-wide evangelism movements weren't working; they were focusing on going all-in, going too big too fast. Instead, Lausanne reminded us to start small, with the individual.

Jesus was God incarnate. Surely, he could have made a big splash if he wanted to. Yet, he didn't come as a rich ruler, a Roman centurion or a member of the Jewish Sanhedrin. Any of these positions would have given him tremendous social and political power to enact broad based changes. Instead, Jesus began small with a few disciples in the villages of Nazareth and Galilee (John 1:46). He chose twelve of the most unlikely and seemingly uninfluential individuals one could find (Matt 10). As people's lives were changed, these small changes were multiplied out into the surrounding towns and villages. Even after his crucifixion, the movement expanded, eventually outgrowing its Jewish roots. It brought the same transformation to the Greek and Roman cultures as well. Jesus started a movement which changed the world—but he started small.

Jesus understood that a direct change to Judaism would have created a strong backlash, producing little lasting change. Instead, knowing the social systems, he utilized a leverage point. He started producing small changes in the lives of a few. Jesus taught his disciples to do the same, by looking for "persons of peace" (read how Jesus sent out his disciples in John 10 and Matt 10). These 'worthy people' were special individuals who welcomed Christ's message and then shared it with their families and friends. Jesus didn't tell them to go into a village and hold a crusade, instead, Jesus taught his disciples to find individuals who would multiply their impact.

The Gospels and the book of Acts are full of stories where persons of peace fanned the flame of change up through various social networks: Zacchaeus passed the message on to a large group of tax collectors and influential people (Luke 19:10), the Centurion introduced these changes to his family and servants (Matt 8:5–13), the Gerasene demoniac, (a particularly unlikely agent of social change), brought the gospel to the ten most influential cities of Israel and the Jordan (Mark 5), and the woman at the well brought change to her community (John 4). Acts 19 shows how this same process impacted the entire province of Asia within just two short years.

DON'T DESPISE SMALL BEGINNINGS

I know an experienced ministry leader who had a good sized ministry that needed a breath of new life. Before getting started, he wanted the organization to move forward in unity. He used 1 Corinthians 1:10 as his guide: let "there be no divisions among you, but that you be united in the same mind and the same judgment." "We must be unified in these changes," he thought.

As with most groups, there were a few who passionately agreed with him on the changes he wanted to see happen. But there were also an equal number who passionately resisted any change at all. Since he desired unity, he decided he would only move forward when everyone moved forward together. He failed to realize that some people easily embrace change, while others won't commit till see it in action. A better route would have been to start with those willing to make a change, and realize that it would take a while for the others to get involved.

If innovations are successful, they will be contagious. Others will follow in time. Unity means we love each other despite our differences. It doesn't mean we all do the same thing. Don't be afraid to start small. Start by finding a few individuals willing to form an innovation team. Begin applying these principles on a small scale.

I know of a similar story with a much different ending. A house church pastor felt God was telling them to plant eight new churches in just three short years. The pastor felt the first job was to pass the vision on to the congregation. Yet any attempt to mobilize the church resulted in strong resistance. A few influential elders replied, "If God told you to start these new churches, why hasn't he told us? Look at how little love there is in our church. Why should we plant more churches? We must focus on discipleship first. Then we'll have something worth reproducing."

The pastor knew they were in for a long, drawn-out struggle, which they would never win. Instead, this pastor sought consensus that the church should grow. This was a point upon which everyone agreed easily. Then the pastor sought consensus that a small group within the church be given permission to try church planting as a method of achieving that growth. If the efforts were successful, the church would continue the efforts. If, however, they were unsuccessful, the church planting group would stop. The church achieved unity, even while still holding a diversity of views. Certainly there were a few elders feeling that the church planting effort would fail, but they consented to the idea, 1) because they agreed with the greater vision, and 2) they felt it was better to "fail" with a small group than to take down the whole church with this crazy idea. Permission was given to move forward.

Instead of seeking complete unity through a unanimous decision, the second pastor focused on creating unity through group consensus. Too many people think that unity in requires everyone to be in unanimous agreement. This couldn't be further from the truth. Consensus allows for a much greater diversity of perspectives and ideas while creating agreement upon a larger picture or on a core principle (Senge 2006). When people reach consensus, they agree to support decisions, not because they agree upon all the details and individual actions, but because they agree to the greater good which the group is trying to achieve. They agree to allow diversity of strategies or viewpoints for the sake of reaching a shared vision of the future. Consensus based decision making creates space for innovation to occur. Unanimous decisions seek conformity, which often stifles creativity. In many cases unity through consensus is much more powerful than being unanimous.

God blessed the consensus reached in this small house church, and they quickly planted a new house church. It grew quickly and many of the new Christians were deeply committed to growing in Christ. In fact, these new Christians were growing much faster in their discipleship and mutual love for each other than the original church. They were also on fire for starting more churches. Seeing the success of the small experiment, the elders blessed the group to plant more churches. At the end of three years, the pastor had seen a total of nine new churches planted.

Change is a risky endeavor. Planting eight churches seems like a tall order, especially when some aren't even happy with the one they have. Starting with an experiment of planting just one new church is much easier. Since it was an experiment, it was nonthreatening, and didn't need unanimous agreement by the entire group. They learned a lot with their first church plant, which helped each successive church plant happen much more smoothly. They learned as they moved forward. Changes multiplied upwards. Starting small had seemed slow; yet it was amazing how fast the remaining churches were planted. In the end, they were planting several churches at once.

The Bible reminds us not to despise the days of small beginnings (Zech 4:10). The temptation to "go big or go home" is tremendous; North American culture doesn't necessarily lend itself to starting small. This isn't to say that big visions are bad. Many times, however, it is better to start small, then find ways to multiply our efforts.

One word of caution: It's important not to start too many experiments at once. You don't want to be scattered in too many directions. Innovation and experimentation doesn't mean we start running off in all directions so that we lose our organization's special strategic focus (Collins 2005). Innovations should reinforce your organization's central theme. They should produce synergy with existing projects, propelling the organization forward, rather than diverting energy away from the organization's reason for existing. Similarly, you should not define your strategic focus so narrowly that individuals don't have any room to truly innovate (Pfeffer and Sutton 2006). Leadership must learn to allow thought diversity within the organization's central theme (Daft 2008). This may initially seem threatening to some leaders. Begin by reinforcing your organization's values, purpose, and core competencies, but don't get caught up defining rules or boundaries (Collins 2005). Give people some room and see what they do.

FAILING FORWARD

Not all innovative experiments will succeed. Learning anything new assumes a certain amount of risk. A child cannot learn to ride a bike unless the child is also allowed to fall down. You could say that falling down is an important and necessary part of learning to ride a bike. A lot of times, people learn more from falling down than they do from succeeding. When we learn from falling down, we fail forward (Oster 2011).

Ty Cobb is one of the best baseball players ever, yet even Ty Cobb still fails to get a hit over 60 percent of the time. If we focused on his failures, we'd miss what an amazing ball player he became. Failure shouldn't be seen as failure, especially if it helps us move forward toward our goals. Leaders must treat their team members with this attitude, giving them space to make and learn from mistakes, without fear of being reprimanded.

When I was working as a consultant, I sold training packages worth over ten thousand dollars each. One month was particularly slow, our paychecks would be delayed again, and the company desperately needed sales. I came up with an idea. I approached our best customer, certain I'd land a huge sale. Unfortunately, my great plan backfired. This customer was irate, and cancelled their existing contract. Our CEO called me into his office. I took a deep breath before I walked in the door, certain I'd lose my job. The CEO sat me down and asked me, in detail, everything that happened. I explained my good intentions, and what went wrong, and why. I had resigned myself to the fact that I was about to lose my job, so I didn't get defensive. His response surprised me: "Don't stop experimenting. Go back and try something bigger next time. You'll probably end up making even bigger mistakes in the future, but you must promise me never to make the same mistakes again." I couldn't have been more surprised. While I saw my "failure" as a disgrace, he saw it as an opportunity to learn and grow. He understood our organization needed innovation to grow out of our struggles, and he was worried I'd lose my initiative as a result of this set-back. Instead of being fired, I was motivated and empowered. His response has stuck with me and encouraged me even after beginning full time ministry.

PUTTING IT ALL INTO PRACTICE

This book has discussed a number of tools to help you make sense of the future and what it may hold. Preceding chapters have also taught you a number of the skills necessary to help you successfully navigate these turbulent waters. Hopefully, you've been practicing with these tools as you've learned them. If so, you'll have a big head-start towards your next challenge. If you haven't, now will be a great time to take a step out of the boat and get started.

In order to start putting these tools to work for your organization, you'll need to put together a team of people to walk through the process. The Bible says, "Two people are better than one, because they can reap more benefit from their labor." (Eccl 4:9, NET). Your team should represent a cross section of the organization so that you incorporate wisdom gained on the front lines.

Teach your team about mega-trends and how to spot changes happening in our world—even changes which may not have a clear, immediate impact on your organization. Collecting these scan hits should be a continuous process which these individuals continue to do on their own. Look for interesting trends, news bytes, decisions being made, or emerging issues. Think about and record how these could impact all the various individuals and organizations operating in your environment. You can use a group email or a note-taking application that allows shared notes to make a central repository of these scan hits. Set aside time regularly to review what you are learning.

After assembling the team, set aside half a day or a day to explore organizational assumptions. Look over your present strategies and identify the assumptions upon which they are built. Look for weak or vulnerable points in your strategies.

What assumptions could suddenly change? What assumptions may not be true? Then take some time to brainstorm scenarios that could kill the organization and its strategies. Identify the scenarios or assumptions that need to be addressed in order to make the organization stronger and more resilient. Identify areas that require more research.

Now you can begin developing various impact maps and scenarios. Set aside a half day or more with your team. Start by looking over some of your more interesting scan hits. Discuss some potential impacts on your organization and strategy. Which ones seem particularly interesting? What might be some similar events which could have a significant impact on your organization? Which ones have the potential to bring tsunamis of change across your environment?

Choose several of these scenarios, then break people up into groups to develop impact maps, one per group. Be sure to push the teams to explore impacts out to the fourth and fifth levels. What insights do you learn? What opportunities and challenges need to be addressed? What new capabilities, opportunities, or challenges might exist? What else would be necessary for each of these to emerge? Bring the groups back together to discuss the impact maps as a large group. Be sure to check yourselves.

Now you are ready to develop scenarios. From the scan hits and impact maps, discuss a number of plausible futures. Narrow these plausible futures down to four or five. Assign each of the plausible futures to a team to develop the scenario. Press the teams to set horizons far enough into the future so that you are not just extrapolating current events. Press them to think deeper. Press them to think farther. Get them to look for higher and higher level capabilities. Look for breakthrough ideas and new perspectives. Write the scenarios in the past tense; imagine you are in the future and you are recording how various events came to pass. Afterward, have the team write down the leading indicators for each scenario.

One of these scenarios should include the "preferable future." What type of future would be most beneficial to your organization? What does it look like? What new capabilities will have been developed? Make sure to press yourselves to think out far enough. Get a clear picture of what this future looks like, then start discussing: what are all the pieces needed for your organization to arrive at this future? What aspects of the present environment must your organization manage in order to help this future emerge? Again, be sure to write in the past tense.

After all the scenarios have been written down, take the time to read and discuss them. What do you learn about the future? What surprises you? What seems plausible now that didn't seem plausible before? What new challenges or opportunities are waiting for you? How does your organization need to adapt? What new strategies must you adopt?

As we've discussed in various examples, such meetings often bring a tremendous amount of creativity and clarity. Success is not predicting or foretelling the future accurately. Success is knowing what must be done to be successful, regardless of what specific future emerges. Scenarios are about helping you prepare and be strategic.

Scenarios should be revisited every six months to a year, or whenever significant changes happen in the environment. The object of the exercise is keep the organization focused upon the trends and changes happening in the environment, as well as to help organizations identify key challenges and opportunities. Such knowledge empowers us to create informed plans that will make a significant impact on the future.

As such, the scenarios and impact maps should stimulate prayer and actionable tasks. The question must be answered: "What, then, must we do?" The hope is that through the process, the organization will become sensitized to changes happening in the environment. Over time, your organization will grow smarter, more able to interpret the signs of the times, and know how to respond.

FINAL WORDS

I hope that by this time you have a clearer understanding of the broad changes happening in our world and how these changes are changing world mission. The changes are much broader than the glimpse I've shared here. I pray you take these tools to uncover and track even more of these changes. Likewise, I hope you've become convinced that our old methods won't continue to work in the new, emerging reality of tomorrow. I've worked diligently to describe a few of the tools which can help you dream about what tomorrow's world will look like. I pray God will lead you into finding your place within that strange new world.

The future will require a special kind of leadership. Leaders need to express a Christ-like love to their people, while reinforcing organizational vision and values. Then, they must create space for individual expression through experimentation, while providing guidance that empowers individuals to grow from their mistakes.

I believe the Spirit of God is calling out to us: "No one puts new wine into old wineskins. If they did, the skins would burst and the wine would run out" (Mark 9:17). "Do not focus on the past. Behold, I am about to do something new" (Isa

43:18–19). "Look among the nations and wonder. See and be astounded. I am doing a new work, which you wouldn't believe, even if I told you" (Hab 1:5). "I have plans for you, good plans for a future filled with hope" (Jer 29:11). "This is my command, be strong and very courageous!" (Josh 1:7,9).

If we simply drew a line from the past to the future, Columbus would have never sailed the Atlantic; Kennedy would never have put a man on the moon; NASA would never have put a probe on Mars. Neither would Carey have dared take the gospel to India, or Taylor to inland China. If God simply drew a line from our past, he would have never sent his Son. God created you to be creative (Oster 2011). Innovation is in your nature. The Great Innovator himself deposited a divine spark within you, his earthly vessel. And as to how we use that divine spark, he will one day call us to account (Matt 25). May we use the creativity God gave us in a way that brings transformation and lasting impact for the gospel; even to the remotest places of the Earth.

BIBLIOGRAPHY

עֶדְיָ, הֶעְדָ. In *Enhanced Strongs Lexicon*. Woodside Bible Fellowship. הָנִיב, 1995.

Abulleil, A. *Personal Conversation*. Pittsburgh, PA: Aliah, Inc., 1995.

Accenture. *Driving Successful Transformational Change through Journey Management*. http://
www.accenture.com/us-en/outlook/Pages/outlook-online-2012-driving-successful
-change-through-journey-management.aspx (accessed: March 22, 2012).

Al-Hajjaj, M. *Bronchial Asthma in Developing Countries: A Major Social and Economic Burden*.
Washington, D.C.: US National Library of Medicine, 2008.

Allee, V. *The Future of Knowledge: Increasing Prosperity through Value Networks*. Burlington, MA:
Elsevier Science, 2003.

Allen, R. *Missionary Methods: St. Paul's or Ours, a Study of the Church in the Four Provinces*. London:
Robert Scott, 1912.

Alliance SCP. *The Omega Course: Saturation Church Planting Manual One*. Charlotte, NC: The Alliance
for Saturation Church Planting, 2008.

Alter, A. "Inspired by Starbucks: Charismatic Pastors Grow New Flocks Overseas, Using Satellites, DVDs
and Franchise Marketing to Spread their Own Brand of Religion." *The Wall Street Journal*.
http://online.wsj.com/article/SB121331198629268975.html (accessed September 19, 2013).

American Bible Society. *State of the Bible in 2013*. New York, NY: American Bible Society. http://www
.americanbible.org/state-bible (accessed June 24, 2013).

Amoako-Attah, A. "Efficacy of Clove (syzygium aromaticum (1.) merr and perry) Powder as a Pro-
tectant of Groundnut Kernels in Storage." *African Journal of Food, Agriculture, Nutrition
and Development* 11 (2011). http://www.ajfand.net/Volume11/N06/ Amoak09835.pdf
(accessed September 19, 2013).

Arango, T. "How the AOL-Time Warner Merger Went so Wrong." *New York Times*. http://www.nytimes
.com/2010/01/11/business/media/11merger.html?pagewanted=all&_r=0 (accessed
December 17, 2013).

Argyris, C. "Initiating Change that Perseveres (Initiating Change: Theory and Practice)." *American
Behavioral Scientist* 40, no. 3 (1997): 299–310.

Associated Press. "U.S. Embassy: Beijing Air Quality is 'Crazy Bad.'" *USA Today*. http://usatoday30
.usatoday.com/news/world/2010-11-19-beijing-air-pollution_N.htm (accessed September
19, 2010).

Barna Group. "5 Myths about Young Adult Church Dropouts." https://www.barna.org/teens-next -gen-articles/534-five-myths-about-young-adult-church-dropouts.

Barone, T. "Giving Trend Shows 'New Normal'—Lower." *California Southern Baptist Convention.* http://www.csbc.com/csb/article319973c5108635.htm (accessed February 7, 2012).

BBC. "China Decries Shenyang Pollution Called 'Worst Ever' by Activists." http://www.bbc.com /news/world-asia-china-34773556 (accessed March 16, 2106).

Beaubien, J. "WHO Warns of Zika Virus's 'Alarming' and 'Explosive' Spread." NPR.org. http://www .npr.org/sections/goatsandsoda/2016/01/28/464690737/who-warns-of-zikas-alarming -and-explosive-spread (accessed March 15, 2016).

Bell, R. *Love Wins.* New York, NY: HarperOne, 2011.

Bingham, J. "Recovery Far off for Families as Disposable Income Sees Biggest Drop for 25 Years." *The Telegraph.* http://www.telegraph.co.uk/news/politics/spending-review/10146720 /Recovery-far-off-for-families-as-disposable-income-sees-biggest-drop-for-25-years.html (accessed September 18, 2013).

Bishop, P. *Framework Forecasting: Managing Uncertainty and Influencing the Future.* Huston, TX: University of Huston, 2005.

Bitgood, K. Personal Phone Conversations and Correspondence with Bitgood. 2013

Blackaby, R. *Experiencing God.* Kindle Edition. Nashville, TN: B&H Books, 2013.

Blake, J. "When Christians Become a 'Hated Minority.'" CNN http://religion.blogs.cnn.com/2013/05/05 /when-christians-become-a-hated-minority/ (accessed June 24, 2013).

Boa, K. "Leadership Qualities: Double-Loop Learning." *Bible.* http://bible.org/seriespage/double -loop-learning (accessed August 6, 2011).

Borthwick, P. *Western Christians in Global Mission.* Downers Grove, Il: InterVarsity Press, 2012.

———. Personal Phone Conversation with Paul Borthwick. Date: 12/11/2013.

Bosch, D. *Transforming Mission.* Maryknoll, NY: Orbis Books, 1991.

British Council. "Bangladeshi Students Win the International Virtual Enterprise Challenge 2013 with Community-Based Handcraft Enterprise." *The British Council Date.* http://www .britishcouncil.org/learning-skills-for-employability-international-challenge-2013 -winning-team-2013.htm (accessed September 18, 2013).

Buckley, C. "China to Ease Longtime Policy of 1-Child Limit." *The New York Times.* http://www .nytimes.com/2013/11/16/world/asia/china-to-loosen-its-one-child-policy.html?_r=0 (accessed December 23, 2013).

Burke, W. *Organization Change, Theory and Practice, 3rd ed.* Thousand Oaks, CA: Sage Publications, 2011.

Canton, J. *The Extreme Future: The Top Trends That Will Reshape the World for the Next 5, 10, and 20 Years.* New York: Dutton, 2006.

Cavanagh, G., and M. Bandsuch. "Virtue as a Benchmark for Spirituality in Business." *Journal of Business Ethics,* 2002.

Bibliography

Censky, A. "Surging College Costs Price out Middle Class." CNN Money. http://money.cnn.com
/2011/06/13/news/economy/college_tuition_middle_class/ (accessed November 27, 2013).

Center for the Study of Global Christianity. "Christianity in its Global Context, 1970–2020: Society, Religion, and Mission." Gordon Conwell Theological Seminary. http://www.gordonconwell.com/netcommunity/CSGCResources/ChristianityinitsGlobalContext.pdf (accessed December 5, 2013).

Chen, X. "Higher Iron Ore Prices Positively Affects Shipping Rates." Market Realist. http://marketrealist.com/2013/08/higher-iron-ore-prices-positively-affects-shipping-rates/ (accessed August 19, 2013).

Clinton, T., and G. Sibcy. *Why You Do the Things You Do: The Secret to Healthy Relationships.* Nashville: Thomas Nelson, 2006.

CNN. "What is Bitcoin?" *CNN.* http://money.cnn.com/infographic/technology/what-is-bitcoin (accessed November 19, 2014).

CNNIC. "Statistical Report on Internet Development in China." *Internet Network Information Center.* http://www1.cnnic.cn/IDR/ReportDownloads/ 201302/P020130221391269963 814.pdf (accessed August 22, 2013).

Colegrove, A. "School Addresses Facebook Rumors." *WSAZ HD.* http://www.wsaz.com/newswestvirginia/headlines/School_Addresses_Facebook_Rumors_135711533.html (accessed December 15, 2011).

Collins. *Good to Great and the Social Sectors: A Monograph to Accompany Good to Great, Why Some Companies make the Leap . . . and Others Don't.* New York, NY: Harper, 2005.

Comhina. "Un Puente a los No Alcanzados." http://www.comhina.org/sitio/ (accessed May 22, 2004).

Corbett, S., and B. Fikkert. *When Helping Hurts: How to Alleviate Poverty Without Hurting the Poor—and Yourself.* Chicago, IL: Moody Publishers, 2009.

Cornish, E. *Futuring: The Exploration of the Future.* World Future Society. Kindle Edition, 2004.

Crabb, L. *Inside Out.* Colorado Springs, CO: NavPress, 1992.

Crosby, R. A Pentecostal Growth Explosion—Over a-fourth of Christendom. Patheos. Date Accessed: http://www.patheos.com/blogs/robertcrosby/2012/05/a-pentecostal-growth-explosion-over-a-fourth-of-christendom/ (accessed May 24, 2012).

Cummings, T., and C. Worley. *Organization Development & Change* (9th ed.). Australia: South-Western /Cengage Learning, 2009.

Daft, R. *Essentials of Organizational Theory and Design.* Mason, OH: South-Western College Publishing, 2003.

———, and P. Lane. *The Leadership Experience.* Mason, OH: South-Western, Cengage Learning, 2008.

Davila, T., M. Epstein, and R. Shelton. "Making Innovation Work." In *The Light Prize: Perspectives on Christian Innovation,* edited by Oster, G. Virginia Beach: Positive Signs Media, 2011.

Dewar, J. A. *Assumption-based Planning: A Tool for Reducing Avoidable Surprises. RAND studies in policy analysis)*. New York: Cambridge University Press. http://assets.cambridge .org/97805218/06534/frontmatter/9780521806534_frontmatter.pdf (accessed February 9, 2012).

Dinmore, G., G. Segreti, and E. de Sabata. (2012). Investigators Probe Cruise Ship's Italy Routes. Rome, Italy: Financial Times. Accessed from http://www.ft.com/cms/s/0/cb4fcc0c -41f6–11e1–9506–00144feab49a.html#axzz11I25nFbs (accessed February 3, 2012).

Draper, E. "Bible Translators Hope to Have Every Language Covered in 15 Years." Denver, CO: The Denver Post, June 22, 2010.

Drucker, P. *The Practice of Management*. New York: Harper & Row Publishers, 1954.

———. (1985). "The Discipline of Innovation." *Harvard Business Review* 63 no. 3, 67–72.

Economist. "Offshoring Your Lawyer: Outsourcing Can Cut your Legal Bill." *Economist*, Dec. 10, 2010. http://www.economist.com/node/17733545 (accessed September 18, 2013).

Eisenberg, E., Goodall, H. Jr., & Trethewey, A. (2010). *Organizational communication: Balancing Creativity and Constraint*, 6th ed. Bedford. St. Martin's: Boston.

Elllis, B. "Average Student Loan Debt Nears $27,000." CNN Money. http://money.cnn.com/2012/10/18 /pf/college/student-loan-debt/index.html (accessed September 18, 2013).

Esteve, E. "Smartphone Shipment Explosion Sustained by $50-$75 devices, Mostly in China." http://www .design-reuse.com/industryexpertblogs/32386/smartphone-shipment-explosion.html (accessed September 18, 2013).

Fox, S. "Technology Changing the Way We Practice Religion." Science on NBC NEWS.com http://www .nbcnews.com/id/38126658/ns/technology_and_science-science/t/technology-changing -way-we-practice-religion/ (accessed September 18, 2013).

Friedman, T. *The World is Flat: A Brief History of the Twenty-first Century*. New York, NY: Farrar, Straus and Giroux, 2005.

Gartner Group. "Gartner Says Worldwide PC, Tablet and Mobile Phone Combined Shipments to Reach 2.4 Billion Units in 2013." Engam, UK: Gartner Group. http://www.gartner.com /newsroom/id/2408515.

Gary, J. "The Future According to Jesus: A Galilean Model of Foresight." *Futures*, 40 (2008): 630–42.

———. "The Post-Church Letters: Voices from 2020." Church Executive. http://churchexecutive. com/archives/the-post-church-letters-voice-from-2020 (accessed December 10, 2013).

———. Personal correspondence. Virginia Beach, VA: Regent University, 2012.

———. Interview. Virginia Beach, VA: Regent University, 2013.

Gladwell, M. The *Tipping Point: How Little Things Can Make a Big Difference*. New York, NY: Little Brown and Company, 2000.

Glenn, J. C. "Futures Wheel." In *Futures Research Methodology* v. 3.0 CD-ROM. American Council for the UNU, 2009.

———. "Scenarios." In *Futures Research Methodology* v. 3.0 CD-ROM. American Council for the UNU, 2009.

"Globalization" (2013). In Merriam-Webster.com. http://www.merriam-webster.com/dictionary (accessed September 18, 2013).

Goleman, D. *Primal Leadership: Realizing the Power of Emotional Intelligence.* Boston: Harvard Business School Press, 2013.

Goodall, H. Jr, and S. Goodall. "Communicating in Professional Contexts: Skills, Ethics, and Ways to Peak Experiences." In *Dialogue, Theorizing Difference in Communication Studies,* edited by R. Anderson, L. Baxter, and K Cissna. Thousand Oaks, CA: Sage, 2006.

Gordon, A. *Future Savvy: Identifying Trends to Make Better Decisions, Manage Uncertainty, and Profit from Change.* New York: American Management Association, 2009.

Greenberg, A. "Silk Road Reduced Violence in the Drug Trade, Study Argues." Wired. http://www.wired.com/2014/06/silk-road-study/ (accessed November 19, 2014).

Greenfield, S. "Mobile Technology Changes Your Brain Claims Neurologist." *International Business Times* (2012).

Grondahl, P. "Human Trafficking, Undocumented Workers Part of Guilderland Homicide Investigation." *Times* Online. http://www.timesunion.com/local/article/Evidence-technicians-return-to-seen-of-4-killings-5813957.php#photo-6984070 (accessed November 6, 2014).

Gu, Wei. "Smog Darkens Shanghai's Prospects for Becoming a Global Financial Center." *Wall Street Journal.* http://online.wsj.com/news/articles/SB10001424052702303932504579253174051857950 (accessed December18, 2013).

Gyes, G. "Career Perspectives of Young Adults." Belgium: European Working Conditions Observatory. http://www.eurofound.europa.eu/ewco/2009/02/BE0902039I.htm.

Hackman, M. Z. and C. E. Johnson. *Leadership Communication Perspective.* Long Grove, Ill: Waveland Press, Inc, 2009.

Halal, W. "Forecasting the Technological Revolution." Techcast. http://www.sciencedirect.com/science/article/pii/S0040162513000346.

Hamel, G., and L. Välikangas. "The Quest for Resilience." *Harvard Business Review* vol. 81, no. 9 (September, 2003).

Hannagan, T. *Management: Concepts & Practices* (5th ed.) Harlow, England: Prentice Hall, 2009.

Handy, C. *The Age of Paradox.* Boston, MS: Harvard Business School Press, 1994.

Hawthorn, N. *The Scarlet Letter.* Boston: Ticknor, Reed & Fields, 1850.

Henderson, H. "Personal Conversation with Heidi Henderson." *Mission to the World.* (2013).

Hesselbein, F., and P. Cohen. *Leader to leader (LTL): Enduring Insights on Leadership from the Drucker Foundation's Award-winning Journal.* San Francisco, CA: Jossey-Bass, 1999.

Hickman, B. Personal Conversation with Bert Hickman. South Hamilton, MA: Gordon Conwell Theological Seminary, 2013.

Hines, A., and P. J. Bishop. *Thinking about the Future: Guidelines for Strategic Foresight.* Washington, DC: Social Technologies, 2006.

HRSA. "Collaborative Improvement & Innovation Network to Reduce Infant Mortality." Washington, DC: US Department of Health and Human Services. http://mchb.hrsa.gov/infantmortality /coiin/ (accessed September 18, 2013).

Holling, C. S. "Understanding the Complexity of Economic, Ecological, and Social Systems." *Ecosystems* 4, no. 5 (August 2001): 390–405. http://www.tsa.gov/assets/pdf/PanarchyorComplexity.pdf.

Hudson, N. "The Greatest Human Migration." Topeka, KS: UTNE. http://www.utne.com/community /thegreatesthumanmigration.aspx (accessed August 17, 2013).

"Innovate." Merriam-Webster. http://www.merriam-webster.com/dictionary (accessed September 5, 2014).

Jenkins, P. *The Next Christendom: The Coming of Global Christianity.* New York: Oxford University Press, 2002.

Jokinen, T. "Global Leadership Competencies: A Review and Discussion." *Journal of European Industrial Training* 29, no. 3 (2005): 199–216.

Jurkiewicz, C., and R. Giacalone. "A Values Framework for Measuring the Impact of Workplace Spirituality on Organizational Performance." *Journal of Business Ethics* 49 (2004): 129–142.

Kalson, S. "Pittsburgh Named Most Livable City Again." *Pittsburgh Post-Gazette.* http://www.post -gazette.com/neighborhoods-city/2010/05/04/Pittsburgh-named-Most-Livable-City-again /stories/201005040289 (accessed December 18, 2013).

Kopp, C. "Amazon Faces Hurdles in Chinese e-reader Market." *USA Today.* http://www.usatoday .com/story/tech/2013/06/11/amazon-china-kindle-yahoo-tmall/2411259/ (accessed September 18, 2013).

Kotter, J. *Leading Change.* Boston, MA: Harvard Business School Press, 1996.

Kroll, L. "Megachurches, Megabusiness." *Forbes.* http://www.forbes.com/2003/09/17/cz_lk _0917megachurch.html (accessed September 23, 2013).

Langer, E. *The Power of Mindful Learning.* New York: Perseus Publishing, 1998.

Laurent, A. "Chinois de France: ne veut rien dire." Slate. http://www.slate.fr/story/23827/chinois-de -france-ne-veut-rien-dire (accessed September 27, 2013).

Lausanne Movement. "The Lausanne Covenant." Lausanne. http://www.lausanne.org/en/documents /lausanne-Covenant.html (accessed September 26, 2013).

Leclaire, J. "Pentecostals Growing with Church Plants." Charisma News. http://www.charismanews .com/us/33103-pentecostals-growing-with-church-plants (accessed May 22, 2014).

Lee, D. "Facebook Plans Satellite 'in 2016.'" BBC. http://www.bbc.com/news/technology-34451081 (accessed March 15, 2016).

Lucero, B. "Are Steam Washing Machines Worth It?" Yale Appliance. http://blog.yaleappliance .com/bid/83826/Are-Steam-Washing-Machines-Worth-It-Reviews-Ratings (accessed September 26, 2013).

Ma, Wayne, and Te-Ping Chen. "Beijing's Bad Air Days, Finally Counted." *Wall Street Journal.* http:// blogs.wsj.com/chinarealtime/2014/04/14/beijings-bad-air-days-finally-counted/ (accessed May 21, 2014).

MacDonald. "10 Minutes with David T. Olson." Religion News. http://www.religionnews.com/index .php?/tenminutes/10_minutes_with_david_t_olson1/ (accessed December 30, 2012).

MacMillan, P. *The Performance Factor: Unlocking the Secrets of Teamwork.* Nashville, TN: Broadman & Holman Publishers, 2001.

Magee, J. Personal Conversation with Jim Magee, GMI. Colorado Springs, CO: Global Mapping International, 2013.

———. Presentation at MissioNexus Conference, Philadelphia. Colorado Springs, CO: Global Mapping International, 2013.

Manjoo, F. "I Want it Today: How Amazon's Ambitious New Push for Same-day Delivery will Destroy Local Retail." *Slate.* http://www.slate.com/articles/business/small_business/2012/07 /amazon_same_day_delivery_how_the_e_commerce_giant_will_destroy_local_retail _.html (accessed December 20, 2013).

Mattson, C. *The Village Drill: Executive Summary.* Gambrills, MA: Freeman Institute. http://www .freemaninstitute.com/water.htm (accessed September 11, 2013).

Marion, D. "Global Water Shortages Grow Worse but Nations have Few Answers." *Scientific American.* http://blogs.scientificamerican.com/observations/2013/08/01/global-water-shortages/ (accessed September 18, 2013).

McGrath, B. *Blackwell Manifestos: The Future of Christianity.* Malden, MA: Wiley, 2002.

"Megacity." Wikipedia. http://en.wikipedia.org/wiki/Megacity (accessed September 19, 2013).

Miller, D. L. *Discipling Nations* (2nd ed.). Seattle, WA: YWAM Publishing, 2001.

Mitroff, I. and E. Denton. *A Spiritual Audit of Corporate America: A Hard Look at Spirituality, Religion, and Values in the Workplace.* San Francisco, CA: Jossey-Bass, 1999.

Modis, T. "Life Cycles: Forecasting the Rise and Fall of Almost Anything." *The Futurist* (September-October, 1994).

Moltmann, J. "The Presence of God's Future: The Risen Christ." *Anglican Theological Review* 89, no. 4. (2007): 577–88.

Murray, B. "Latino Religion in the U.S.: Demographic Shifts and Trends." Sacramento, CA: Hispanic Evangelical Association. www.nhclc.org (accessed February 11, 2013).

Newport, F. "Americans' Church Attendance Inches up in 2010: Increase Accompanies Rise in Economic Confidence." Gallop, Inc. http://www.gallup.com/poll/141044/americans-church-attendance -inches-2010.aspx (accessed December 10, 2013).

Newport, F. *God is Alive and Well: The Future of Religion in America.* New York, NY: Gallop Press, 2012.

Nsiah-Gyabaah, K. *Urbanization, Environmental Degradation and Food Security in Africa.* Montreal, CA: Global Environmental Change Research Community, 2012.

O'Brien, W. *Choosing a Future for U.S. Missions.* Pasadena, CA: William Carey Library, 1998.

Operation World. *Operation World Website.* Colorado Springs, CO. Global Mapping International, 2013.

Oster, G. *The Light Prize: Perspectives on Christian Innovation.* Virginia Beach: Positive Signs Media, 2011.

PA Refugee Resettlement Program. "Demographics and Arrival Statistics." US Department of Health and Human Services. http://www.refugeesinpa.org/aboutus/demoandarrivalstats/ index.htm (accessed November 27, 2013).

Parish, D. "The Fourth Era of Modern Missions." Benton, KY: World Missions & Evangelism, Inc. http://worldmissionsevangelism.com/the-fourth-era-of-modern-missions/ (accessed November 27, 2013).

Patton, C. M. "What is the "New Calvinism" and Are You a Part of It?" *Credo House Ministries.* http://www.reclaimingthemind.org/blog/2010/04/what-is-the-new-calvinism-and-are-you-a -part-of-it/ (accessed January 2, 2014).

Peddy, S. *The Art of Mentoring—Lead, Follow and Get out of the Way.* (2nd ed.). Houston: Bullion Books, 2001.

People's Daily. "China Encourages Mass Urban Migration." People's Daily. http://english.peopledaily .com.cn/200311/28/eng20031128_129252.shtml (accessed September 18, 2013).

Pfeffer, J., and R. I. Sutton. *Hard Facts, Dangerous Half-truths, and Total Nonsense: Profiting from Evidence-based Management.* Boston, MA: Harvard Business School Publishing, 2006.

Plaut, V., H. Markus, H., J. Treadway, and A. Fu. *The Cultural Construction of Self and Well-Being: A Tale of Two Cities.* Sage.

Polak, F. *The Image of the Future.* Amsterdam: Elsevier Scientific, 1973.

Polaris Project. "Hotline Statistics." http://www.polarisproject.org/resources/hotline-statistics (accessed May 21, 2014).

Porras, J. I., and R. C. Silvers. "Organization Development and Transformation." *Annual Review of Psychology* 42, no. 1 (1991): 51–78.

Porter, E. *Why Traditional Western Agencies Must and are Changing.* GA: MissioNexus, 2013.

Price Waterhouse Coopers. "Talent Mobility 2020." pwc.com/managingpeople2020 (accessed June 12, 2013).

Ramesh, R. "400,000 Children will Fall into Relative Poverty by 2015, Warns IFS." *The Guardian.* http://www.theguardian.com/society/2011/oct/11/children-poverty-institute-fiscal-studies (accessed September 18, 2013).

Reverend, R., and R. Tannenbaum, "A Dialog on Dialog." *Journal of Management Inquiry* 1, (1992): 43–55.

Rogers, E. *Diffusion of Innovations.* Glencoe: Free Press, 1962.

Ronsvale, S. "Few Churchgoers Tithe, Study Says." *USA Today*. http://usatoday30.usatoday.com/news/religion/2008-05-31-tithing-church_N.htm (accessed December 10, 2013).

Ronsvalle, J., and S. Ronsvalle. *State of Church Giving through 2011*. Champaign, IL: Empty Tomb, Inc, 2013.

Rubin, J. Z, D. Pruitt, and S. H. Kim. *Social Conflict: Escalation, Stalemate, and Settlement* (2nd ed.). New York: McGraw-Hill, 1994.

Rundle, S. "Does Donor Support Help or Hinder Business as Mission Practitioners? An Empirical Assessment. *International Bulletin of Missionary Research* (2014).

Safo, P. "Six Rules for Effective Forecasting." *Harvard Business Review* 85, no. 7/8 (2007): 122–31.

Sanders, J. O. *Spiritual Leadership: Principles of Excellence for Every Believer*. Chicago, IL: Moody Publishers, 2007.

Sanders, T. I. *Strategic Thinking and the New Science*. New York: The Free Press, 1998.

Seipp, D. "Strategic Foresight and the Future of World Mission." *Lausanne Global Analysis* 4, no. 1 (2015).

——. "The Changing Environment of World Mission: Six Areas of Importance." *EMQ* 49, no. 2, (2013): 292–96.

——. "On Confucius and Chinese Leadership Development." *Unpublished.*

Senge, P. *The Fifth Discipline: The Art and Practice of the Learning Organization*. New York: Random House Digital, 2006.

——. A. Kleiner, C. Roberts, R. Ross, R. and B. Smith. *The Fifth Discipline Fieldbook: Strategies and Tools for Building a Learning Organization*. New York: Doubleday, 1995.

Schultz, W. "Environmental Scanning: On the Common, or Garden Variety, Environmental Scan." *Infinite Futures*. http://www.infinitefutures.com/essays/fs8.shtml (accessed July 2, 2013).

——. "The Foresight Fan: Systematic Approaches to Foresight." *Kings Fund European Symposium*. http://www.infinitefutures.com/essays/publichealth/foresightfan.shtml.

Schumpeter, J. *The Theory of Economic Development*. Cambridge, Massachusetts: Harvard University Press, 1934.

——. *Capitalism, Socialism and Democracy*. London: Routledge, 1942.

Shayon, S. "Kodak Emerges from Bankruptcy with Focus on Digital Imaging, Commercial Printing." *Brand Channel*. http://www.brandchannel.com/home/post/2013/09/04/Kodak-Emerges-From-Bankruptcy-090413.aspx (accessed December 20, 2013).

Shaw Jr, M, and E. Wan. "The Future of Globalizing Missions: What the Literature Suggests." *Global Missiology*. www.enochwan.com/english/articles/pdf/The percent20Future percent200f percent20Globalizing percent20Missions.pdf (accessed February 25, 2013).

Shiels, J. "Liturgical Worship is Dead." *Wandering Pilgrim*. http://a-wandering-pilgrim.blogspot.com/2011/07/liturgical-worship-is-dead.html (accessed December 20, 2013).

Siebeck, M. *The Early Christians in Ephesus from Paul to Ignatius*. Grand Rapids, MI: Wm. B. Eerdmans Publishing, 2004.

Sola, K. "Beijing's Smog Alarms Public, But Data Shows India's Air Quality Is Far Worse." (accessed March 16, 2106).

Stetzer, E. "Multi-site Evolution." *Christianity Today.* http://www.christianitytoday.com/edstetzer/2013 /june/multisite-evolution.html (accessed December 10, 2013).

Surrat, G, G. Ligon, and W. Bird. *The Multi-site Church Revolution: Being One Church in Many Locations.* Grand Rapids, MI: Zondervan, 2006.

Tagg, J. "Double-loop Learning in Higher Education." *Change* 39, no. 4, (2007): 36–41.

Tansey, S. *Business, Information Technology and Society.* New York, NY: Routledge, 2003.

Tansey, S, G. Darnton, and J. Wateridge. *Business, Information Technology and Society.* New York, NY; Routledge, 2003.

Taunton, L. "Listening to Young Atheists: Lessons for a Strong Christianity." The Atlantic. http://www .theatlantic.com/national/archive/2013/06/listening-to-young-atheists-lessons-for-a -stronger-christianity/276584.

Taylor, C. *Modern Social Imaginaries.* Durham: Duke University Press, 2004.

Tuckman, B. "Developmental Sequence in Small Groups." *Psychological Bulletin* 63, no. 6 (1965): 384–99.

United Nations Department of Economic and Social Affairs. "World Urbanization Prospects, the 2011 Revision." *United Nations.* http://esa.un.org/unup/ (accessed September 18, 2013).

Urbanek, K. *Cuba's Great Awakening: Church Planting Movement in Cuba.* Dallas, TX: Church Starting Network, 2012. [Kindle edition].

United States Environmental Protection Agency. "Particulate Matter (PM)." EPA. http://www.epa .gov/airquality/particlepollution/ (accessed May 21, 2014).

US Census Bureau. "2012 National projections Updated May, 2013." US Census Bureau. http://www .census.gov/population/projections/ (accessed September 18, 2013).

US Dept. of Health and Human Services. "Human Trafficking into and within the United States: A Review of the Literature." ASPE. http://aspe.hhs.gov/hsp/07/humantrafficking/litrev/index. pdf#search=Human Trafficking (accessed November 6, 2014).

UNCCD. "A Stronger UNCCD for a Land-Degradation Neutral World." United Nations Convention to Combat Deforestation. http://www.unccd.int/Lists/SiteDocumentLibrary/Publications /Stronger_UNCCD_LDNWorld_issue percent20brief percent2004_09_13 percent20web .pdf (accessed September 19, 2013).

Venere, E. *Environmental Policies Matter for Growing Megacities.* West Lafayette, Indiana: Purdue University, 2013.

Yi, L. *Cultural Exclusion in China: State Education, Social Mobility and Cultural Difference.* London: Taylor & Francis, 2008.

Walker, M. "Five Trends Changing the Future of Missions: Predictable Future Trends Based on Current Influences." Schaumberg, IL: Baptist Bulletin. http://baptistbulletin.org/?p=16785 (accessed January 2, 2014).

Wang, H. "Food Safety Tops Public's Concerns." *China Daily.* http://usa.chinadaily.com.cn /china/2013–08/21/content_16909023.htm (accessed September 19, 2013).

Warren, R. *The Purpose Driven Life.* Grand Rapids, MI: Zondervan, 2002.

"Washing Machine." Wikipedia. http://en.wikipedia.org/wiki/Washing_machine (accessed January 14, 2014).

"Water." Water. http://water.org/water-crisis/water-facts/water/ (accessed September 18, 2013).

Werbel, J., and S. M. Demarie. *Aligning Strategic Human Resource Management and Person-Environment Fit: A Strategic Contingency Perspective.* Academy Of Management Proceedings & Membership Directory, 2001.

Winseman, A. "U.S. Evangelicals: How Many Walk the Walk?" Gallop. http://www.gallup.com /poll/16519/us-evangelicals-how-many-walk-walk.aspx (accessed June 24, 2013).

Winston, B. E. *Be a Leader for God's Sake: From Values to Behaviors,* rev. ed. Virginia Beach, VA: Regent University, School of Leadership Studies, 2002.

Winter, R., and S. Hawthorne. *Perspectives on the World Christian Movement,* third ed. Carlisle, UK: Paternoster Press, 1999.

Wolf, A. *The Transformation of American Religion: How We Actually Live Our Faith.* Chicago: The University of Chicago Press, 2003.

The World Bank. "Results Profile: China Poverty Reduction." The World Bank. http://www.worldbank .org/en/news/feature/2010/03/19/results-profile-china-poverty-reduction (accessed September 18, 2013).

World Futures Society. *Horizon Mission Future.* Bethesda, Maryland: World Futures Society.

World Health Organization. "Reliable Evaluation of Low-level Contamination of Food—Workshop in the Frame of GEMS/Food-EURO." Kulmbach, Germany (2013): 26–27.

Wycliffe, Inc. "Strength in Numbers: Communities Translate the Bible." *Wycliffe Blog.* http://wycliffe .org.uk/blog/tag/crowdsourcing/ (accessed December 30, 2013).

Zylstra, S. "Southern Baptists Lose Almost 1,000 Missionaries as IMB Cuts Costs." *Christianity Today.* (accessed March 16, 2016).

INDEX